STO ✓

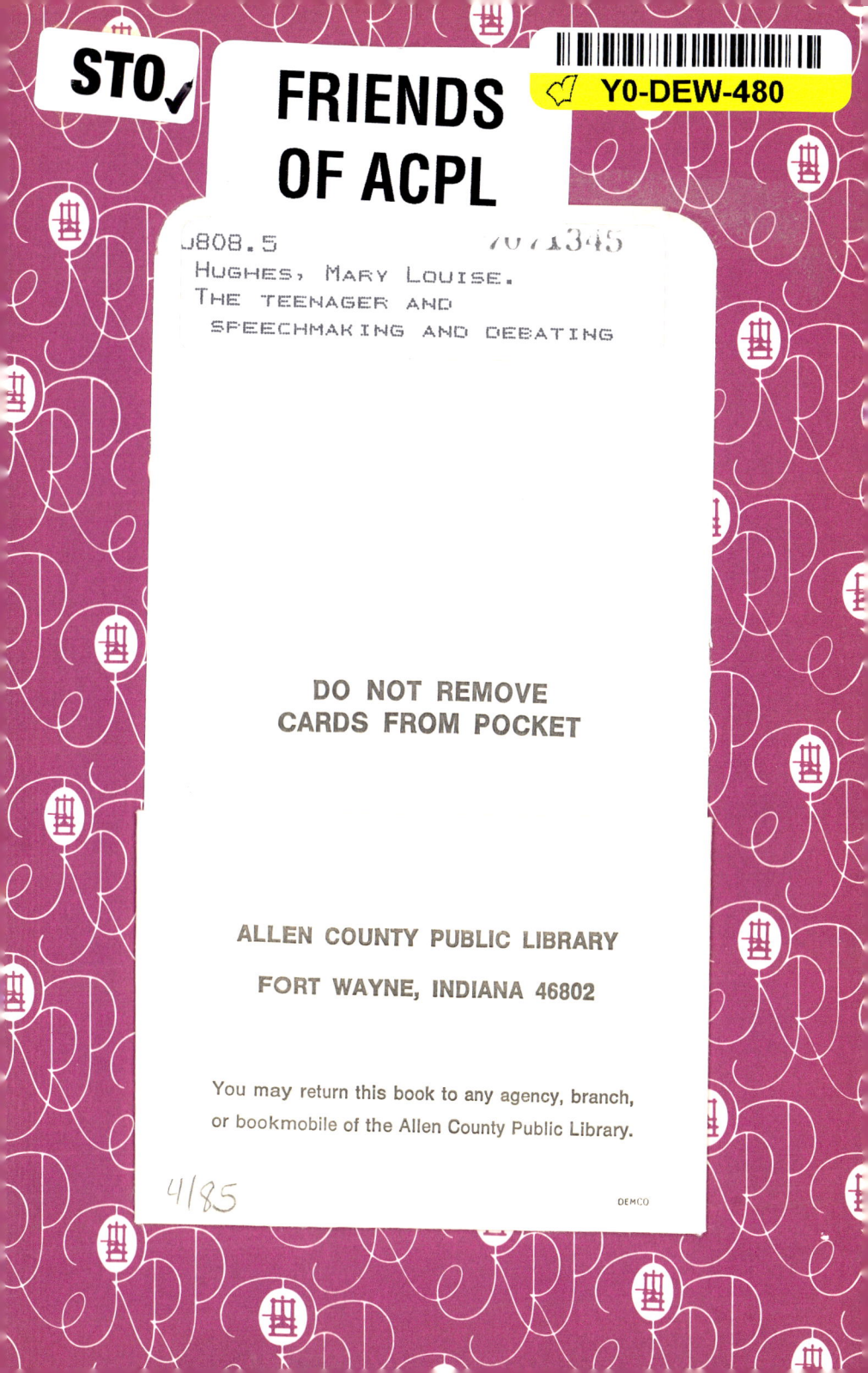

FRIENDS
OF ACPL

Y0-DEW-480

J808.5
HUGHES, MARY LOUISE.
THE TEENAGER AND
SPEECHMAKING AND DEBATING

7071345

DO NOT REMOVE
CARDS FROM POCKET

ALLEN COUNTY PUBLIC LIBRARY

FORT WAYNE, INDIANA 46802

You may return this book to any agency, branch,
or bookmobile of the Allen County Public Library.

4/85

DEMCO

THE TEENAGER AND SPEECHMAKING AND DEBATING

THE TEENAGER
AND
SPEECHMAKING
AND DEBATING

MARY LOUISE HUGHES

RICHARDS ROSEN PRESS, NEW YORK, N.Y. 10010

Library of Congress Catalog Card Number: 69-11716

Published in 1969 by Richards Rosen Press, Inc.
29 East 21st Street, New York, N.Y. 10010

Copyright 1969 by Mary Louise Hughes

All rights reserved. No part of this book
may be reproduced in any form without written
permission from the publisher, except by a reviewer.

Manufactured in the United States of America

About the Author

Mary Louise Hughes has been interested in speech training during her years of teaching. Her experience ranges from pre-school Head Start groups, through primary, elementary, junior- and senior-high-school classes in speech, debate, theatre, radio, and television. She has directed one university theatre production.

She earned her educational bachelor's degree from Teachers College, Cincinnati, Ohio, and taught on the elementary level.

Upon entering the secondary field of education, she specialized in oral communication subjects, obtaining a master of arts degree in teaching speech and theatre from St. Louis University. She has taught speech subjects in Chicago, Illinois; Columbus, Hamilton, and Cincinnati, Ohio.

After writing and producing a children's television series, she was released from full-time classroom duty to work further in the development of educational television. At present, she is cooperating with the Norwood, Ohio, school system in the preparation of an educational television program.

At a journalism class conducted by members of Theta Sigma Phi at the University of Cincinnati in 1967, she was encouraged by Emalene Sherman to write for magazines. Since that time she has had articles published in *Parent-Educator* and *Sunday Visitor*.

Besides teaching speech and writing for educational magazines, she operates an amateur radio station at the MARY Studio, Cincinnati.

She holds membership in state and national speech, theatre, radio, and television organizations.

*Dedicated to
my mother
and my father.*

Acknowledgments

I would like to thank the following talented teens for permission to quote speeches and remarks: Alison Maddux for her speech, *What's to Be Done About Dope?;* the champion Ohio debate team from Purcell High School consisting of Steve Rehling, Chuck Luken, Paul Sylvester, and Chip Zoller; Alison Maddux and Jerry Romer for photographs; Ken Shatto and Jim Bailey for photography.

Contents

Introduction	13
I. Speaking and Listening	21
II. Speechmaking Skills	29
III. Party Line: Initiate Speech Parties	52
IV. On Your Mark: You Against Blank Paper	71
V. Get Set: You Against the Written Paper	87
VI. Go! You Before Your Audience	105
VII. Argumentation and Debate	112
VIII. New Worlds Await You	132
Appendix	139

Introduction

Spring is covering our land. A youthquake is bubbling up from New York to Los Angeles; from Detroit to Dallas. Twenty-four million boys and girls between the ages of 13 and 19 are growing up in America! By 1970, experts tell us, half the population of the United States will be under 25 years of age.

A national asset of 24,000,000 vibrant, vivacious teens is a tremendous gross national product. New wealth fills the human treasury. A real renascence is near!

America awaits you, teens! America has hopes that your generation will prove to be its greatest blessing.

America has given you beauty. You are the best-groomed, best-scented, best-tinted generation yet to appear in the human family. Yet, cosmetic beauty is only "lotion deep." A query in a teen magazine asks, "Why do you think it all happens on the outside?" The question demands an answer. *Your* answer. *Do you sound as beautiful as you look?*

The power of sound brought down the walls of Jericho and has served as the keystone of every civilization in the history of man. The cost of cosmetics to make you look beautiful has soared into nine-digit numbers, but what investment has been made to make you *sound* beautiful?

Your personality is fully revealed only when you speak. It is on an intellectual level that you reach the minds and hearts of men. Physical attraction is not enough. You must *sound* as beautiful as you *look*.

14   *The Teenager and Speechmaking and Debating*

Do you sound as beautiful as you look?

If you wish to become an attractive speaker, you begin with the first requirement—a desire to improve. The second basic requirement you already have—a voice. You began your speech-making career at the time you cooed your first syllable. Your ecstatic parents thrilled at your first achievements in sound.

Sound, and its human production, always seems something of a miracle. The improvement of sound is a continuing miracle. Perhaps you have grown up, as have most of today's 24,000,000 American teens, without much attention to vocal beauty. Yet, if you are to accomplish the great things America hopes you will, you must be skilled in the art of speaking.

Your voice is a channel for your thoughts. Words are mirrors reflecting the inner you. Cosmetics achieve a "painted-on" you; speech reveals the real inner you. Beauty must be deeper than externals. Beauty, to be real, must come from the heart.

Billy Graham feels that the big problem facing our nation is "disease of the heart." If you wish to become an effective speaker, begin with a heart charged with positive, dynamic love.

To be a convincing speaker, you need faith. Faith is a virtue by which you believe in God, in people, and in yourself. You feel affection for God. Your life is a gift from Him . . . and all your talents and possibilities.

You believe in yourself. You believe in dreams, ideals, visions. You also believe in *work*. Man is creative, but always "in the sweat of his brow." You review the achievement of such great men as Thomas Edison and heed his own critique: "one percent inspiration; 99 percent perspiration." Inspiration and perspiration are the ingredients of success. But success begins with a vision of faith.

With faith in your heart, then, set out to speak to others. Speech is the channel by which your faith will flow into the lives and hearts of others.

Hope, too, is part of speaking. Through your own hope, you radiate life. Speakers seek to instill hope in the minds of their hearers, just as physicians seek to bring health to their patients.

16 The Teenager and Speechmaking and Debating

Speech is the divine gift of the human being.

Hope flows from faith. It is an element of your *inner* strength and beauty. Hope must reside in your thoughts and flow through your words.

Along with faith and hope, comes love. The mightiest force of all is love. Through love, you unfold your personality into the kind of person you want to be.

True self-love means that you champion the right to be yourself—your best self. Dare to be your best, true self. Set your own pattern. Make your own decisions. Respect yourself. Follow the advice of the wise and ancient Socrates: "Know thyself."

Know your strengths and your weaknesses; your relation to the universe; your potentialities; your circle of influence for good.

Learn to love yourself, to forgive yourself, to encourage yourself. With this attitude of love, you can experience the feeling of love for others. Then, prepare to speak with love, to others.

We hope you will become an effective speaker. In the words of Henry Higgins, in *My Fair Lady,* "Remember that you are a human being, with sound and the divine gift of articulate speech; that your native language is the language of Shakespeare and Milton and the Bible."

True, it may be "the worst of times." But with 24,000,000 young people, there is great prospect that it may become "the best of times."

Speech is of the essence of democracy. A nation that claims to be democratic is as strong as its speakers are powerful.

And so, future speechmakers of America, we salute you. You are the springtime visiting our land. You are our 24,000,000 reasons for hope!

THE TEENAGER AND SPEECHMAKING AND DEBATING

CHAPTER I

Speaking and Listening

What happens when you speak? Speech is an involved process. It is sometimes represented as a moving cycle. You are familiar with a bicycle or a motorcycle. Each is a device with rotating wheels. A bicycle has two wheels. A motorcycle has its wheels powered by a motor. A speech cycle resembles the whirling motion of a bicycle or a motorcycle.

Speech arises in the mind and begins a spinning motion through the power of thought. The one producing the thought looks for a word to express the thought. The thinker, or speaker, is *coding* it into verbal language. After selecting a word, he sounds or phonates it into "speech." The speaker sends the sound out onto the air waves. Through the air it travels to the ear of the listener. The listener is a *receiver;* the speaker is a *sender.*

The receiver, or listener, picks up the sound. He examines the word or words and proceeds to *decode* the message. He is getting the meaning out of the words. He is attempting to understand the thought in the mind of the speaker. For this thought process to take place, there must be a pause. This pause is a period of silence.

The sender does not send out a further message until he gets a response from the receiver. He now waits in the role of receiver to pick up a return message. The first receiver now becomes the second sender. His return message is called *feedback.*

This process is known as the *cycle of communication.* You

will recognize it as the process that takes place when you have a conversation with someone.

Communication has many forms. The smoke signals of the Apache, the starter's pistol in a foot race, the Morse Code, and various systems of writing are just a few examples of the many different systems of communication used by man. Unquestionably, speech is the system that man found most efficient and convenient.

The amount of intelligence exchanged in speech is vastly greater than that produced by books, newspapers, and magazines. The areas of the world's most highly developed civilizations are those where speech is highly developed.

The phenomenon of speech is worth careful study. It is worthwhile because this study provides useful insights into the nature and history of human civilization.

Electrical experts study the built-in human communication system to develop better and more efficient electronic communication systems. Speech—the cycle of communications—is also an important study in the just-emerging field of man-to-machine communication. We all use automatons such as the dial telephone and the automatic elevator, which either get their instructions from us or report to us on their operations. Frequently, they do both. Examples are the highly complex digital computers used in scientific laboratories. In designing communication systems or "language" to link man and machine, it proves especially useful to have an understanding of the simplest communication cycle—the pattern of man-to-man speech.

In the communication cycle, thoughts are coded into words. Words are arranged into phrases in correct grammatical order. The brain directs the speech organs to deliver the message. Impulses are sent along motor nerves to the muscles of the speech organs—the tongue, teeth, lips, and vocal cords. Breath supply arising from the lungs passes through the vocal cords into the mouth where the thought-words are molded into specific sounds. These sounds forced out into the air produce minute pressure

SPEAKING AND LISTENING 23

The cycle of communication—speaking and listening!

changes on the surrounding space. We call these pressure changes a sound wave. Sound waves travel between speaker and listener. Pressure changes at the ear activate the listener's mechanism and produce impulses that travel along the acoustic nerve to the listener's brain. In his brain, a considerable amount of nerve activity is already taking place, and this activity is modified by the nerve impulses rising from the ear. This modification of brain activity, in ways we do not fully understand, brings about comprehension of the speaker's message.

Activity takes place on three levels—in the areas of thought, words, and sound production. The cycle of communication rotates many times during the process of one conversation. From speaker to listener, from receiver to sender; words travel at varying speeds. Imagine, if you can, the volume of words being produced at this moment—in conversations, by telephone, in conferences, discussions, in court trials, by radio, television, and satellite.

Thoughts expressed in speech have greater influence on the lives of men than thoughts expressed—or written—on paper. Speech is instantaneous, while written communication is not.

The power of the spoken word has long been recognized in the world of human affairs. Adolf Hitler wrote in *Mein Kampf*:

"Every great movement on this globe owes its rise to the great speakers of the day."

Marshall McLuhan notes that electronic communication devices have made the world a "global village." The powerful eye of the TV screen and the voice of the commentator make life "pure information."

Man's ability to use his built-in communication system, however, is at an all-time low ebb. Eleanor Roosevelt, on the occasion of the launching of the satellite Echo I, remarked:

"We now have a satellite on which to communicate, but where can we find the people who know *how* to communicate?"

A communications era demands communications experts. As part of the American youth explosion you, as teens, should excel in the art of intelligent and expert communication. You must become skilled in the art of speaking. How?

What happens when you listen? When you listen, you complete the first cycle in the act of communication. As a speechmaker, you will be confronted with the surprising fact that people do not know how to listen. They may come to hear you speak, but they are not necessarily good listeners. The burden of making people listen will be thrown entirely upon you as the speaker.

Listening breaks down so badly that businessmen have resorted to confirming spoken messages, either by contact, phone, or written statements. One New York business firm's byword is: "Don't say it. Write it."

Some people admit they can sit and look at a person and never hear a word he says. Statistics show that usually about two months after listening to a person talk, the average listener will remember only about 25 percent of what was said.

Listening may well be our most important element of personal communication. Usually about 70 percent of our time is spent in verbal communication, 9 percent in writing, 16 percent in reading, 30 percent in talking, 45 percent in listening. Most of an adult's information is gained through listening. The poorly trained ear works overtime. People spend 70 to 80 percent of their time on the telephone. Half of this is spent listening. A company pays an employee 35 to 40 percent of his salary for listening on the telephone, to say nothing about listening in other situations.

In political elections, people receive their information mostly from what they hear. Newspaper and magazine information supplies 27 percent, experts tell us, radio and television 58 percent. Decisions are made by listening to what other people say about subjects with which we ourselves do not have contact. The life of a man on trial in court, or his sentence to prison, depends on the persuasive speech of his lawyer and the listening ability of the members of the jury. Their decision rests on a cycle-of-communication process. No wonder the Greeks thought it so important!

Listening is as important as speaking.

SPEAKING AND LISTENING

Speaking and listening are important in everyday life. The very news we hear daily depends very much on the cycle of communication. It is reported by people listening to people, or people listening to machines. Reporters receive much of their information from oral interviews, from speeches of individuals, or from press conferences. If journalists are to be fair and accurate, they must be the best of listeners.

Authorities in industry are concluding that sometimes good or bad listening can even make or break a business. Large firms are bound together by their communication systems, and industry is spending hundreds of millions of dollars to make these systems work. At the same time, many industrialists know that good business communication is a dying cause if the people involved are poor listeners.

These situations may result from the fact that so little is being done in the educational process in the speaking-listening area. The study of English is largely concentrated on reading ability. Listening skills are unthought of as a development area. These may be skills you will have to develop on your own. A student in the art of speech is also a student in the art of listening.

"Listen!" "Now get this straight!" "Pay attention!" These common commands do not necessarily *produce* listening. Listening is achieved only if attention is given to the message of the speaker. It is the obligation of the speaker to understand the area of listening and to create good listening through good visual presentation.

Listening is apparent if the speaker has the listener's eye. There he will see a glint of recognition. Perhaps a nod of the head will accompany the look of understanding. Facial expression may also register pleasure, even a smile. This reaction of the listener to the speaker is very important. It sets up rapport. It completes the cycle of communication.

Listener response stimulates the speaker. It says to him: "You're coming in clear. I understand you. I agree with you. Go on. I can take more!" These are positive reactions and are the spark needed by the speaker to enable him to loosen up, to keep going, to try harder. Negative reactions make the road rough for the person talking. He must struggle to overcome the bad reactions, to change them in his favor. The way the listener responds to the speaker gives the latter some indication of his success in the process of communication.

The expert speaker will want to know about the role of the listener. Listening, too, is an art. It follows set rules.

Your listener judges you first on the basis of *integrity*. He is asking himself: "Is he or she sincere, telling the truth, making accurate statements, drawing correct conclusions?" An entire thought process such as this, and more, can take place during the one-minute span it takes you to enunciate 125 words—the normal speaking rate.

Though the speech process is comparatively slow, the thought process is much more rapid. So your listener can take in your 125 words and have time left over to take in other pieces of information. He may note your physical appearance, objects in the room, people about him, the temperature of the room, lighting facilities, or perform myriad other mental tricks. He is giving you attention, but he has time left over to give other things attention as well. It is in this block of interest that you will perhaps develop *visuals* later on.

At present, we know your listener is judging you as a work of art, whether he knows it or not. His attention will naturally follow:

1) an attractive introduction;
2) stimulating, information-filled development;
3) resolution into a course of action in the conclusion.

Certainly, to have had his attention he must have had the "light" to follow you from the beginning—the light of understanding your words, the light of your logical reasoning, the light of enough sound to carry the message.

CHAPTER II

Speechmaking Skills

How do you improve? Put your best self forward! Give yourself an *inner personality test.* You are a good boy or girl. You are a teen with hopes for a better personality. You are young with visions of a better America.

A good person is not always necessarily perfect. A good person always wants to grow; to try to be even better. Accept yourself, just as you are, with your possibilities or limitations. Do not blame others for your failure. Begin to teach yourself. Have faith in your destiny as a future speaker. Champion the right to be yourself without being aggressive or domineering. Lean on others, but not to the point of losing your own ideals or your own identity. Respect others and respect yourself. Forget yourself. Help others. Experience the joy of doing for others, even if it costs you personally. In this way you will experience inner joy. This will spill out, like liquid gold, into your smile and your conversation.

Cut all offensive words out of your vocabulary; all tale-bearing; all unkind remarks. Find good things to say about people. Do not use your tongue to cut or injure others.

Learn to smile. Brush it on with your cosmetics. Learn laughter and simplicity from your younger friends—the children. Be real. Think for yourself. And work! Work with all the energy you have.

Study art—the art of speechmaking. Art, first of all, is of the intellectual order. Its action consists in imprinting an idea on

Through exchange of ideas, you come to an appreciation of the inner person.

SPEECHMAKING SKILLS

matter. We acquire skill through repeated actions; through exercise and use of a power.

The world seeks beauty. In this age of hi-fi and stereo, it seeks beauty of sound as well as visual beauty. In the Miss America contests, finalists are given just one test of attractiveness. They are asked to talk briefly about themselves before a panel of judges. They may be sensational in appearance, but a thin quality of tone in their voices and thinner selection of words in their statements will quickly disqualify them as beauty queens. The world today looks for teens who *sound* as beautiful as they *look*.

If you would become a good speaker, become interested in art—the art of sound. Beauty is essentially an object of the intellect as well as of the eye, for the intellect delights in knowing. The natural place for beauty is in an intellectual world. The art of speaking belongs to the realm of the intellectual, but also to the art of the senses. In man, the senses serve the intellect. The intellect depends upon them for knowledge.

Speechmaking is an art. It is a performing art. It is an active art. Activity is opposed to boredom. In this richest land on earth, boredom in the United States is as big a problem as poverty.

In human activity, speaking or speechmaking is classified in the realm of fine art. *Logic* was the early name for speechmaking. Just as the musician arranges intellectual sounds in his soul; just as the mathematician arranges numbers, the logician, or speaker, arranges concepts or thoughts. His oral or instrumental expression cause these thoughts to pass into sonorous material.

Speechmaking, then, as a fine art is classified in the realm of making and is governed by an end, rules, and values. The work of art has been conceived before being made; it has been prepared, brooded over, ripened in the mind before taking form. Expressed, it retains the color and savor of the spirit.

In other words, your art, your speechmaking, reveals the inner you. As an artist in words, you are a student seeking to express the true, the good, and the beautiful.

A smile adds sparkle to your words.

The beautiful may be defined as that which, being perceived, pleases. "Being perceived" implies senses. "Pleases" indicates a higher realm, the intellect. Intellectual pleasure, or delight, is the delight of knowing. Speech is one of the simplest channels by which we know.

Beauty has three ingredients: integrity, proportion, and radiance or clarity. Integrity, or truth, illumines. Proportion, or relationship of parts, pleases. Clarity, or intelligibility, delights. The intellect knows, understands, comprehends.

Art indicates delight, but it also implies drudgery. It is through work on matter that art aims at delighting the spirit. Imagination is the chief purveyor of art. Art is fundamentally inventive and creative. It is the faculty of producing, from preexisting matter, a new creature, an original being, capable of stirring, in turn, a human soul.

Artistic creation does not copy God's creation; it continues it. The artist, weaving new elements together in an original pattern, consults God in making new "things," whether he knows it or not. Nature is the first exciter and first guide of the artist. There he sees truth—things as they exist. There he sees balance and proportion—the relation of one element to another. There he sees clearly—color, texture, shape, form, design.

"The model," said Renoir, "is there only to set me on fire, to enable me to dare things that I could not invent without it."

Translated, all of this means that you, as a student of the fine art of speechmaking, will need a good imagination! Imagination is the ability by which we produce *images* mentally. We see with a mental, or inner eye, as clearly as we see outwardly with a physical eye. By our power of imagination, we arrange elements into new patterns or designs.

As a student in the art of speechmaking, then, you will need to develop and use your imagination. The world in which you live today demands the need to do everything better. Speaking is certainly one of these areas. You must be smarter today. You must meet today's challenge with an ever-increasing ability to think creatively. Conditions have given birth to an absolute need to do everything better—with deeper appreciation and heightened responsibility. This is being overlooked. Some are still trying to solve problems by repetition, imitation, cuteness, sleight-of-hand, or guessing. Many cannot repeat a good idea in a difficult situation because they can't arrive at an original good idea. Glibness replaces creative thinking.

Teens who can think creatively are needed to become new creative forces in our society.

How do you become creative? Think. Reduce problems to their essentials and work your way through them in an organized and imaginative manner. Only hard work produces solutions. How do you get ideas? Think things out—experiment! When a solution pops up, someone will say: "How stupid not to have thought of that!" But the thinking through was the important point. It takes a creative person to *think through the first time*. After that, it's easy.

Work is never easy, but it is less difficult than being wrong from half to three-quarters of the time. Thinking is never easy, but it is the only solution to a problem. Isolate a problem, think it through, identify the leads to its solution, and then work!

Seek the truth! Much is made currently of the glaring inadequacies of our students in linguistic expression—violations of truth. An awareness of the basic tools of research is a must for a speaker.

Build your own personal library. A story in a recent teen publication featured a report on the manner in which a junior-high student had done this very thing. The collection and its use brought her many advantages in home study, as well as a handsome check toward her future education.

Set off a corner of your room and install a few shelves. Suggest books as gifts for your birthday or for other occasions. Include in your collection as many kinds as possible:

SPEECHMAKING SKILLS 35

A speechmaker is a researcher. Withdraw from your friends to a quiet spot as you sort out your facts.

dictionaries   bibliographies
wordbooks   biographies
encyclopedias   books of quotations
anthologies   annual almanacs
histories   indexes

If a personal library is not possible, then make good use of your school or neighborhood library.

Use balance and proportion. As a student of speechmaking, you are working in the realm of art. Next to integrity or truth, you will be interested in the proportion and balance of your work. This implies a relationship of parts. Parts of a speech are usually considered as the beginning, the middle, and the end. Some prefer the terms: introduction, development, and conclusion. A proportion of one-three-one is a good one: one minute, introduction; three minutes, development; one minute, conclusion.

A quotation may be used as your opening sentence in the introduction. It must be lively and dynamic. Your opening sentence is your attention-getter; the hook you throw to "catch a bite." The introduction may state the importance or the timeliness of the subject.

The development moves into more specifics. Important facts are given; usually: who, what, when, where, how, why, with what results.

The conclusion may ask a question: Where do we go from here? It may indicate action: What will you do about it?

Don't overlook clarity! Clarity will result from the type of words you use. Your area of knowledge must overlap the area of knowledge of your listener. In other words, you must use expressions he understands; subjects with which he is familiar. From the known, you proceed to the unknown. You tell him a few more things about things he already knows. Clarity is achieved through language and logical procedure from the known to the unknown.

Clarity is achieved through diction. Your words must be articulated clearly. Be aware of the use of teeth and lips in producing clear and concise sounds.

Clarity is achieved through volume. If your words do not reach the ear, you might as well save yourself all the other efforts of speechmaking. If your volume is too low, your listener will be uncomfortable; he will squint, or grimace. Use enough volume to make the sounds heard.

Improve your thoughts. Your thoughts are expressed in words —the inner you—the real you. Truth is the ultimate goal of speech. Faith, hope, and love are the first requisites of a student pursuing the art of speech.

Speech will flow as a result of your gratitude for the beauty of life and the world about you. Gratitude will prompt you to share your thoughts with those around you. You will see in speech an opportunity to give of yourself: your ideas, dreams, purposes, ideals, principles, and plans.

Speech will flow from your experiences with your fellowman. Will Rogers said: "I never met a man I didn't like." People always listened to the homespun philosophy of a man who liked other men.

Speech will flow from your experience with the world about you. As you travel, you will gather impressions of all things great and wonderful, from jet planes to mountains to cathedrals.

Speech will flow from your desire to laugh. Laughter makes the world go round, and speech calls for laughter. Learn to smile and season your words with smiles, as the day is garnished by sunshine.

Speech will flow from your experiences of every day as you go "idea-hunting" every morning. Speech will flow from your treasury of ideas; from the depth and wealth of your personality.

Speech will flow from a memory filled with happy thoughts, a notebook filled with happy ideas, a communication system filled with happy words.

Only speech can make a complete personality.

Improve Your Words

> "God wove a web of loveliness,
>   Of clouds and stars and birds,
>   But made not anything at all
>   As beautiful as words!"
>
> Anna Hampstead Branch

A word should mean what you intend it to mean. Like Humpty-Dumpty, you should feel that when you use a word, you have selected it with care. It means just what you choose it to mean—neither more nor less!

Words should fit your age—and intelligence. When you were a child, you "spoke as a child," and this was fitting. But when you are a teen, you should speak with words that have outgrown your childhood years.

Words are the clothing for your thoughts. Do yours indicate rags or riches? Like Aristophanes, the ancient Greek comedian, do you feel that "ideas require to be clothed in suitable vesture"?

Make your words lively words. The world of speech is full of empty words, platitudes, clichés, trite, worn-out, dead words. Words are the tools by which you paint your thoughts. They are the threads that form the cloth of your canvas.

Increase your word power. Learn the meaning of new words and check your understanding of familiar ones. Pronounce them aloud and fix their spelling in your mind. Put words into sentences and practice them in private. Finally, assimilate each word by introducing it into conversation and speeches.

Avoid barbarisms, slang, vulgarisms. A barbarism is an inaccurate word.

"You've excelled the speed limit!" shouts the traffic officer. He means *exceeded*.

Verbal sharpness enables you to sense the distinctions between words. In case of doubt, a quick look in the dictionary will set you straight.

A *slang-uage* should never replace a language. Slanguage is coined by the illiterate.

Use simple words. Simple words are clear, understandable words. Simple words are not to be confused with words for simpletons. Great speeches are not a combination of unusual words, but an unusual combination of usual words.

Colorful and meaningful words are expressed in *simile* and *metaphor*.

A *simile* is a short statement in which a comparison is expressed through the use of *like* or *as*.

"As fat as a pumpkin" gives you an immediate sensation of color, size, and shape.

A metaphor *implies* a comparison: "pumpkin-fat."

Gather lists of similes and metaphors from magazines that feature columns of "Flights of Fancy," or "Picturesque Speech." Better still—create your own!

Improve your grammar! Make your sentences stand on their legs and march. Make them slide, skip, jump, turn spins! Flabby sentences start off with a limp and end in a crumpled heap. They begin ". . . And then . . ." "And then . . ." They end ". . . and things like that"; "and everything"; and, "Well, you know what I mean."

Make your sentences simple. Do not overload the sockets. Use plenty of outlets. Use periods to come to a halt. Avoid run-on sentences. Like head-on collisions, they are fatal.

Make use of crisp nouns, colorful adjectives, energetic verbs, timely adverbs.

Clinch your main ideas with climaxes. Before you leave an important point to go on to the next, drive home the sense and significance of your statement with a quotation, an example, or an anecdote.

Everyday clothes are for everyday occasions. Formal clothes fit formal occasions. So, too, with words. Your wardrobe should fit the time and place.

Make use of correct grammatical construction. Construction

Learning to speak is like learning to drive—you must know and follow the rules.

of sentences is as important as construction of buildings. Rules must be followed or your building will collapse.

Replace *and* with transition words. These are words that turn corners for you in switching from one idea to another. Use balanced sentences. They are like teeter-totters. Use the same expression on the second side as you used on the first side.

Observe traffic signs! In speaking, punctuation marks are the traffic signs. A period means a full and complete stop. It is your refueling point. A period gives you time to get new breath if you are the speaker; a time to get the idea if you are the listener.

A comma means yield, slow down, caution. A comma indicates a shorter span for rest.

Quotation marks tell you to change your voice. You are using the words of another.

A question mark indicates a question is being asked. Inflect your voice in an upward intonation.

An exclamation point registers surprise. See that your voice does the same.

A colon means: more to follow. Your voice registers this meaning.

Punctuation marks are to a speaker what traffic signals are to a driver. They tell him when to stop, when to increase or decrease speed, when to change tone, when to change lanes of communication.

Improve your practice: Begin to write what you will say.

It is true, as Francis Bacon remarks, that: "Reading maketh a full man, conference a ready man, and writing an exact man."

Many teens excuse themselves from the exacting task of writing by saying they have no place to write. Compare this statement to the type of writing that has come from a jail cell, or other unlikely place. Martin Luther King Jr. produced some of his best speeches from a jail cot. O. Henry did the same. Oscar Wilde wrote some of his most beautiful stories while in prison.

Speaking, or speechmaking, must be preceded by writing. A library is a good place to do this. It is quiet, and plenty of source

Traffic signs regulate traffic. Punctuation signs regulate speech.

material is available there. In the absence of a favorable place, a future speechmaker must find an available place.

The writing nooks of authors range from under a hair-drying device, to a telephone booth, to an attic or coalbin.

Speechmaking demands accurate and sometimes backbreaking preparation. Ideas can be arranged only in a place that affords peace and quiet. Books of reference are important, a dictionary, books of quotations, newspaper clippings. Plenty of determination is also required, for writers are those who dig into their own minds to rearrange ideas to come up with pleasant and presentable compositions of thought.

While the writer can assign thoughts to paper, and let the reader take it from there, the speaker must go on into the second stage of preparation—committing the written form to vocal form.

To the written message, the speaker must add the exciting and interesting dimension of living sound. He must prepare his voice to transmit the message. He must begin the cycle of communication.

Improve your voice. Your voice, like your thoughts, is a mirror. If a mirror is cracked or distorted, so too will be the image it reflects. If your voice is tense, or drab, or dull, so too will be the thoughts and feelings it projects.

Your voice needs vitality. Speakers without voice training usually talk on one, two, or three tones. You can imagine the monotony of music if only three keys were used in a composition for piano. The voice range encompasses many, many tones.

Tempo and quality are important characteristics of your voice. Words spoken too fast are lost on the ears of the listener.

Vocal quality is the most sensitive indicator of emotion in speaking, and it is least subject to control by the inexperienced speaker. It is very hard to disguise or simulate emotion, because vocal quality always gives clues to one's feelings. Sincerity of emotional expression stems from sincere involvement in the emotion itself.

Improve your voice—like your thoughts—it reflects YOU!

A slower rate of speaking is used in addressing a large audience than in intimate conversation. Complex ideas, statistics, or problems that the audience has not previously considered take longer to grasp than simpler or more familiar statements.

In expressing emotions such as joy and excitement, we usually speak more rapidly than when expressing grief or reverence.

Your voice is the most accurate revelation of yourself.

Improve your diction. Open your mouth wide, just as the dentist tells you. Most Americans suffer from a "closed jaw." Open your mouth as wide as you can. If you hope to be a good speaker, you must be able to open your mouth from the jaws. Your jaws end under the ears. All of this is your mouth. All of this is used in the production of sound. Your mouth opens from jaw to jaw, not just in the lip space.

Vowels are all open-mouth sounds. The widest opening is the long *i* sound. For a good, clear *i* sound, open wide. Otherwise, you will come up with something akin to *ah*. Sounds are molded by the oral or mouth muscles. As you close your mouth more, you get a sound like the *a* in b*a*t. If you strike a certain key on the piano, you get a definite sound. If you form your mouth into a certain position, you get just as definite a sound.

In the *ee* sound, pretend you are stretching a rubber band. Stretch your lips. Your lips are pulled to the side, so that your teeth show.

In the *o* sound, your lips are round; they take on the shape of the letter itself. Long *u* is more nearly "ee-you."

Vowels give richness and beauty to your voice. Prolong your vowels in speaking as in singing.

Consonants should be made clearly. They are produced by the contact, or near-contact of the various organs of articulation: teeth, tongue, lips, throat muscles. They have various names: plosives, fricatives, nasals, and glides.

Articulation may be compared to the process of cutting-out with a scissors. You must cut on a sharp, definite line. The pattern you cut out must have an accurate shape and form.

Plosives are the letters *p, b, t, d, k,* hard *g, dz.* Care must be taken when using a microphone that these sounds are not used too forcefully. The amplification of the microphone will exaggerate the explosion of sound. Some speakers go so far as to avoid words with *p's* especially, wherever possible.

Fricatives are so named because the manner of their production results in a friction-like noise. These are the sounds *f, v,* soft and hard *th.*

Three nasal sounds in English, *m, n,* and *ng* are especially effective when using words with sounds like wind, ring, hum. If the resonators *nnnn* are used, the sound will be very much like a wind sensation. The same is true of the rinnnnggggg of a bell; or the hummmmm of a bee.

Some speakers chew words. Common errors in diction are *senchoo* for *sent you; blesshyoo* for *bless you.* There is a great tendency to merge, or chew, a *t* sound into *ch* before a *y* (I broughtcha this book).

Vowel sounds, then, are more sonorous sounds. They depend for beauty on a wide-open jaw and a forceful air stream rising from the lungs, passing through the vocal box, and, unobstructed, out through the mouth.

Consonants are formed by placing obstructions on the outgoing tone. Vowels give carrying power to the voice.

Through articulation drills, you gain efficiency in opening your mouth, rounding and forming your lips, manipulating your tongue so as to produce clear, crisp, correct speech.

Improve your pronunciation. Pronunciation has two aspects: (1) placing the accent or stress on the proper syllable in the word, and (2) choosing the particular vowel or consonant that is to be used in a given instance. Looking words up in the dictionary will make you certain. Sometimes various pronunciations are given, but there is always a preference. Your speech may be very INT-resting, but it loses value if you say inTERESTing. Check your pronunciation of doubtful words.

SPEECHMAKING SKILLS

Improve your voice quality by improving volume. Volume is the product of the amplitude or extent of the vibration when the factor of pitch is held constant. Amplitude is dependent largely on the resiliency of the vibrating body and on the strength of the activating force that sets it in motion. Volume is also closely related to the distance the sound waves are required to travel.

In the voice, volume is the product of three conditions:

1) the pressure exerted upon the outgoing breath;
2) the efficiency with which the vocal cords vibrate;
3) degree of reinforcement supplied to the tone by the resonance chambers.

Quality of voice enables one to identify a trombone, a clarinet, or a violin when all three are playing the same note, with equal loudness and for the same duration of time. Quality enables one to distinguish the voice of Fred from the voice of Jim, even though both may speak with similar pitch and inflection patterns.

A good speaker will study his voice. As a good pianist insists on an excellent instrument on which to play, a violinist a worthy violin, so a good speaker should be aware of the instrument of his voice.

Begin with God. Prayer is simply a greeting to your Best Friend. Talk to Him as easily as to your most intimate acquaintance.

Greet members of your family in a cheery, pleasant manner. Begin your own *Good Morning Show* at home every day. Say "Good morning" to your father and your mother; your brothers and your sisters. Your greeting will bring a response in the greetings returned to you. Your family should rank first in your circle of friends.

If a "Good morning" seems too formal, think up something original. "A happy day to you!" Or "Happy Tuesday," might be a good substitute—but do greet your family. Greet friends and acquaintances as sincerely and as warmly as you can.

Courtesy is shown in your manner of speech throughout the day. When asking for something at the breakfast table, or over the cafeteria counter, *Please* or *May I?* are appropriate forms. *Gimme* or *I wanna* are vulgarisms. *Pardon me, Excuse me, Please, I'm sorry* are words of an artist interested in the beauty of sound. They should be more natural in the vocabulary of teens than *Get out of my way; Hey, who do you think you are?* and similar expressions. *Thank you* marks you as a person of refinement—a fine arts enthusiast. Examination of speech habits will convince you that the art of speech is indeed virtually a lost or abandoned one in America today.

However, you can do something about it.

Telephone conversation is another area that comes in for attention. While it is normal and healthy for you to wish to talk to your friends, to do so at the inconvenience or danger of others is selfishness. If the world is to be saved, it will be through selfless teens. As Joaquin Miller observed: "The man who lives for self alone, lives for the meanest mortal known." Continued selfishness will produce increased meanness. Telephone conversation, like all speech activity, should be limited to reasonable time allotments. Remember your listener in the cycle of communication. Remember, too, that other people are waiting to communicate.

Teens are not selfish young people. They are merely thoughtless at times. However, recognition of others' needs will prompt them to be courteous and considerate in telephone use.

Go "off the air" at least half of the time to give the cycle of communication a chance to revolve. Some teachers do all the talking in class. This is selfishness. The pupils are entitled to at least equal time. Some parents talk all the time and the teens listen. Some teens talk all the time, and no one listens.

If anyone is emotionally upset, listen sympathetically. If some-

SPEECHMAKING SKILLS

Rehearse means to re-hear many times.

one is angry, let the tirade flow until it is exhausted. Never use the power of speech to hurt others.

Improve your public relations through your power of speech!

What are the listening reactions that help people to talk freely, to open up and give us everything in them? Most of the time the reactions are hard to pin down. Sometimes you need to hear yourself talk out loud. You need someone to listen to you. If you are a good listener to others, you will find others who will be the same for you. We are all sounding boards.

Listening takes courage. Whenever we listen thoroughly to another person's ideas, we open ourselves to the possibility that some of our own ideas are wrong. Most of us resist change, especially when it has to do with altering thoughts that may have been with us since childhood. When we listen, we try to understand the other person's point of view.

As a listener, you will observe people as they talk. Movements or gestures accompany words. Gestures help words to be understood. The spoken word is not communicated in the same manner as the written word. The ears do not work alone. Experts tell us we listen also with our eyes. Words are only a part of communication. The muscles of the body move as well. Temperature shows in the color of the face, the moisture of the hands. Even silence can be eloquent. Self-betrayal oozes from all the pores. The pitch of the voice says something; the way one pauses between words, the speed at which one talks, all indicate a mood or emotion.

In print, a word is a word—black on white. When spoken, a word comes to life. It has a facial expression of its own. The simple word can be altered by simple changes in voice or gestures, each of which may give a new twist to the meaning.

Speakers and listeners, then, have far more to assimilate and work with than readers of the printed page. The speaker works with his ears, eyes, and his whole being. The listener responds in the same way. Speaking is not a passive activity. Listening is equally as active. Both take a great deal of mental energy.

Improve Your Chance for Success

How? Through your study of the art of speaking; your casual, everyday habits of speech; your ability as a listener; your casual, everyday habits of listening.

Work on yourself as an individual, then form some groups to free-lance in the art of speaking.

CHAPTER III

Party Line: Initiate Speech Parties

Planning a party is like planning any other project. There is a desired goal—fun and fellowship and an opportunity for teens to have a good time together. Certain steps are necessary to reach the goal. Invitations must be issued, the party site located, the program planned. All this takes work. It also takes leadership. An alert leader will realize that much more interest in the party can be created if many of the persons who are expected to attend have a share in planning and running it.

A speech party may be something new in your neighborhood. It is intended for those who want to learn to improve their speech skills at the same time they are having "fun." It is an occasion to provide an informal audience for the purpose of practice.

Artists take their easels and go to the woods to paint. Drivers must practice on the roads. Why shouldn't speakers provide occasions—picnics, boatrides, parties—to learn to speak? Those with creative and artistic leadership will have to be the pioneers in the project, especially if "it's never been done before." A beginning effort will result in further ingenious efforts. Select your place, your time, and your group. Tell those invited it is a *speech party*—something new, and quite the fashion!

Like Maria in *The Sound of Music*, begin with something easy. Begin with a *definition* party.

A simple method for giving a definition is fitting the word into a special class or group. Is it a person, place, or thing? Define

PARTY LINE: INITIATE SPEECH PARTIES   53

this person, place, or thing further to describe it more accurately. Then give its function or purpose.

Begin with a simple object. A desk. A desk is a *thing*. Refined, or polished, a desk is further classified as a piece of furniture. Continue the statement, giving its specific use or purpose: A desk is a piece of furniture, at which I do my homework.

You have made your first statement. What next? Where is it located? The answer may be: A desk is usually found in a classroom, or: My desk is in the corner of my bedroom.

Next, think briefly of the age or history of the desk. Was it always there? Did you always have a desk?

The answer: My desk was a birthday gift from my parents.

Of what is it made? It is a maple desk, with four drawers. You are now giving some of its qualities. You are going into a simple description.

End with some generalized statement, such as: A desk is a very handy place to keep books, or write assignments.

Be sure you observe the stop sign—the period—at the end of each complete thought. Do not fill in with *and, ah, um,* or other vocalized pause.

You are beginning to follow a simple outline—the first step in organizing your thoughts and statements.

Subject: Desk
  Definition—who or what? (setting)
  Position—where?
  History—when acquired?   (past, present, future)
  Characteristics—maple   (size, shape, texture,
             drawers   weight, dimensions)
  Generalization—closing thought (usefulness, value)

As an impromptu speaker, when time is very scarce, it is very easy to jot down simple "memory pegs" of such an outline, from which you easily fill in complete thoughts. Be sure, however, to *pause at the end of each complete thought.* This may sound very elementary, but many so-called speakers break this rule repeatedly.

Learn to define! Give the class—is it a person, place or thing? Give the use or purpose—with which, by which, in which, for which.

Put words on slips of paper. Place them in a box or hat. Pass them around. Have each member select one. Try these for beginners:

house   knife   glasses   book   boat   artist

Add others. Encourage each speaker to add his own. Go through the alphabet. Assign topics in *a* one time; *b* the next; down to *z*.

Topics and Titles

If you are a beginner, begin with easy things. Begin with subjects that are familiar to you:

Yourself
   name
   telephone
   address
   school
   subject or subjects you like in school

Be sure to pause at the end of each sentence. A pause means a count of *1-2*.

You, further
   an event of the summer
   a trip
   a picnic
   a visit
   a boat ride

a movie
a book
a hobby

Others
This time, add a title:

A Person I Know

    a fireman   a dentist
    a policeman   a bus driver
    a librarian   a garageman
    a doctor   a mailman

Animals (pets)
a dog, a cat, a bird, a horse, etc.

Quotations and Proverbs

Have fun with quotations and proverbs. You will find them fascinating and thought-provoking. The French have a saying: "Judge a man by his favorite proverbs." We do not give much attention to proverbs or sayings in today's world, but a good speaker will have a few tucked away somewhere in a notebook or in his memory on which he can draw as from a reserve bank account—for security—for preparedness. Always be prepared. Make games of this for your speech clubs—and when you meet, speak. Camera clubs take pictures—art clubs paint pictures. Don't always be on the passive side of entertainment—make your own. Borrow or beg a book of quotations or proverbs. Use them to make your talk interesting and colorful.

Open the book at random, or choose at will. Explain what the words or lines mean to you. See how you can apply it to a situation today, or in your own group. Try to be informative, amusing, original. The ability to form ideas on the spur of the moment will add excellent experience to your public speaking "know-how."

Reduce boredom; stimulate thinking, originality, appreciation. Truth, improvement, encouragement, are the purposes of talking, as opposed to idle, foolish, or depressing talk.

Begin a game of "start talking." Words, topics, titles may be put on slips of paper, in a box or hat, and passed around. Give so much time to get ready. Talk for thirty seconds—have someone keep time. Put back titles. Choose the winner. Next time around, take out a slip and talk for *one minute*. Choose the winner again. Make an opening statement, a few facts, and a closing comment. Timer should give signals, just as on television shows. A good speaker always stays within his time.

The above examples may be considered speeches of information. They are the simplest kind for beginning practice. The next type are a little more difficult. They must follow step-by-step procedure, and are usually called *how-to* speeches. Try yourself on some of these:

Explaining Facts
How to go downtown from where you are now.
How to get to school from your home.
How to find the library.
How to find a specific book in the library.
How to do or make ———.

Speaking is not reading word for word. It is the process of saying words from thoughts. These must be so well formed in your mind beforehand that you know what you are going to say before you get up. You may use an outline and jot down a few hard-to-remember facts . . . but the bulk of the speaking is *speaking* and *not* reading. Let yourself go, so that when you speak you do so as naturally as you talk.

Practice Makes Perfect
Practice every day. To become a skilled pianist you must practice on the piano. To become a skilled speaker, you must

work with your voice, at least ten minutes a day. Walk around a room; talk to yourself; listen to yourself; be at home with yourself.

As you practice, you will notice a growing ease and fluency in word flow. Your ideas will begin to formulate better. Your thought stream will begin to pick up speed.

As you find yourself "taking on" these simple and elementary outlines, begin to deepen and develop more ideas. Make a more extensive outline:

Topic
    Opening sentence:
        definition, timeliness, importance
    Developing points:
        characteristics, kinds, changes, examples, quotes
    Conclusion:
        advantages—disadvantages
    Closing

By this time, you will have overcome stage fright, that paralyzing experience that freezes your thought flow, your word flow, your very breathing. Stage fright exists only if you have not practiced your speech arts daily, either before a few other people, or before yourself. Stage fright is folly. You would not attempt to play a piano before an audience without having trained and practiced daily for many weeks. So in speechmaking, you must train and practice daily. Stage fright is only a form of fear. You can overcome this fear by daily practice.

Conversation

Conversation is the type of speaking in which you engage most. Conversation is an art along with every other type of speaker-listener relationship. But because it is used so frequently, it sometimes does not claim careful attention. Let it come in for some practice at your speech party.

Conversation, first of all, should be kind. If we are using the gift of speech to belittle someone, silence is much more desirable. Shakespeare compares the tongue to a two-edged sword. The Bible tells us we shall have to give an account of "idle" words, that is, words that have no purpose or which accomplish no good.

In conversation, be cheerful. Find the happy things to talk about. Look on the positive side of life. The "every-cloud-has-a-silver-lining" attitude will prompt your words to be happy words.

In conversation, find intelligent or sensible topics to exchange views on. Reading is always a safe and profitable conversation piece.

Each of us wants someone to be interested in us. Conversation is a pleasant way to ask someone about himself. Center attention on the other person more than on yourself. If you try to divert the spotlight to yourself always, the other party to the conversation will soon be disgusted. Think of the other person. Do not ask personal questions; wait until your conversationalist advances information.

Considerate speech is more important than great eloquence.

Begin easy practice in speechmaking by improving your ability as a conversationalist. Remember, kind and helpful words are the rule. Know when to talk and when to keep still. Don't keep still because you are moody or offended. Smile and forget any injury you may have noticed to yourself. Have good manners. Do not interrupt while others are talking. Don't talk with food in your mouth. Suit your conversation to the occasion. Find things of importance to talk about. Prepare several topics for "possible" conversation from your reading or observation. Travel is a good subject for conversation, or exciting experiences you have had.

The student of speech must never forget to listen. People are more interested in their own thoughts than in yours, but do have your own thought to contribute. If their thoughts are gloomy or centered about the world's catastrophes, or personal illnesses, or worst of all the ill reputation of others, use a little "trick" topic to slip in that will turn the trend to more favorable areas.

Conversation art should begin at an early age. It is very sad to see children interviewed on television who do nothing but shake their heads or answer in grunts: *"yeh, nah, dunno."*

Teach younger children how to answer in words and how to put their thoughts into complete word patterns. You will be doing them a great favor as well as preparing them to be good conversationalists. It may be a good idea for a babysitting pastime. Begin with having them use words; then phrases; finally, sentences with a complete pause at the end. Speech parties can be part of children's parties.

The habit of gossiping dangerously and endlessly about others is a fault, or imperfection; a blemish of character. Good speakers do not stoop to it. They try to improve the condition if they find it. Always steer conversation into happy channels.

Practice impromptu speeches. If you have had plenty of practice, you are always prepared for an impromptu speech. It is not so much the speech that is impromptu as the occasion. Many events call for an on-the-spot vocal tribute. A practiced speaker finds no problem in calling up thoughts and phrases to fit any situation. This is part of the reward for his practice in speechmaking.

On an impromptu occasion, if you are asked to give a few words, ask yourself the same questions as for any speech:

"How do I fit into the picture?"
"What is the occasion?"
"What message shall I give?"
"Who is the audience?"
"Who, or what, is the subject of the occasion?"

Memory, too, will serve you well on such an event, for you will quickly be able to recall a line of poetry, a quotation, an anecdote, or example to illustrate your words. Use the same, simple frame of construction—introduction, development, and conclusion.

From your practice in giving short informal speeches on many occasions, you will go sailing through an impromptu occasion with the greatest of ease.

Impromptu speaking is no problem for anyone who has spoken in a warm and sincere manner day by day, in conversation, on the telephone, or before a casual or formal group.

Introductions

Teens, while attractive and friendly, sometimes omit the happy opportunity of introducing friends to each other. Perhaps it's lack of know-how. Practice introductions at your speech party.

There are a few simple rules:

At home, present your teachers to your parents.
At school, present your parents to your teachers.
Present your parents to your school principal.
At home, present your school friends to your parents.
Present younger people to older people.
Present men to women; boys to girls.
Present everyone, except well-known people, to your hostess or to a clergyman.

Mention the most important person by name first: "Mother, this is Peggy Ryan. Peggy, I'd like you to meet my mother."

At school, say: "Mr. Brown (your teacher), may I present my mother and father?"

It is important to give the names of both parties clearly and accurately. Often it is necessary to spell a difficult name, or repeat it two or three times. Name pins are good to use if there are too many new names to remember.

As on all speaking occasions, rehearse introductions beforehand, so as to be at ease when the actual moment arrives.

If you remember the rule, the *most important person first,* or the person you know best first, or the person who belongs in that place first, the rest should be easy. Just don't forget the introduction!

Introductions may be classified, as all speech is, into informal and formal occasions. As you talk casually on some corner, a friend may come into the group who is unknown to the others there. This is a friend of yours. While friendship may be a thing of which poets sing, courtesy in friendship is often overlooked.

"May I introduce Peggy (or Jim), a friend of mine? Peggy (or Jim) is one of my associates in . . . (swim club, tennis club, etc.)."

The greeting, from the one being introduced, may be, "I'm happy to know you," or a simple "Hello." Be sure Peg or Jim is included in the circle as conversation continues. This is true also in a restaurant, at a theatre party, a dance—any occasion on which you meet friends and acquaintances. The demands on a good conversationalist begin with introductions.

Perhaps you are asked to introduce a speaker at school, or at a dinner party. The rules for pleasant introduction require that you know a little about the person you are introducing. You then manage to find some similarity between the subject the speaker will discuss and the interests of the group. This is where your creativity and originality come in. Find out what he is doing that will be of interest to someone you know in the crowd. Jot it down, word it casually but attractively. You are an artist in words. Give two or three good advantageous statements. Follow this with his name. For example:

"Many of us have had an interest in . . . flying for some years. Today we are privileged to have an expert in this field . . . Mr. Orville Wright."

Make visitors feel at home. After your speech of welcome, continue the welcome. Think ahead of things that would make the stay pleasant. Don't overlook rest rooms, cupboards for hats and coats and briefcases. If electric equipment is necessary, find out ahead of time and have it ready. Know how it works yourself in case assistance is needed, or get someone else to do this for you. Hotels are good examples of this kind of attention. Much literature in the rooms tell of service, places to go and visit during a stay in town. If you are a welcome committee of one, provide the same sort of service.

Speeches of farewell. Someone is leaving the group. Reminisce a little about the past without getting sentimental, express appreciation for what the friendship has meant. Plan ahead. A gift may be meaningful, but a gift with words is much deeper and well-received. It's not what you give, but how you give it; the sentiment of the words means as much, if not more, than the actual gift. If you are the person departing, have something ready to say in case you must respond. Express gratitude for friendly associations, what you have learned from all as a group or several in particular. Extend good wishes and hopes to keep in touch. If you have a personal philosophy to share, express it, but always end on the upbeat.

Commemorative events. Anniversaries, family and community: Talk about the people who made the special event possible, personal contributions of time, talent, money; history, purposes, work, accomplishment . . . and best wishes for success in carrying on.

Introduction of speaker. Think of yourself as a go-between, a situation-maker, not as the speaker himself. Find out all you can beforehand about the person you are introducing. If at all possible, talk with him and with people who know him. Track down some reliable biographical sketches, but don't try to use everything you gather together. Don't make your introduction sound like a paragraph from *Who's Who*. If the audience doesn't know much about the speaker, choose information that will identify him, establish his qualifications to speak, and make him liked as a person.

If you can, let the audience see for themselves what kind of person he is by telling an anecdote that puts him in a favorable light. If he is already well known, keep your introduction short and concentrate on the warm sentiments the audience feels toward him.

Above all, be accurate. You may have heard introductions in which the speaker's name was mispronounced or completely garbled. Not every speaker can transform a blunder into a pleasantry. Use some untoward situation as a turning point for your

PARTY LINE: INITIATE SPEECH PARTIES 63

speech. When Rabbi Wise was introduced as Rabbi Mann he joked: "It's a wise man that knows his own name." Someone who fell up the steps began by turning the incident to his advantage. "I hope you noticed I fell up the steps. I don't fall for all my audiences so well." This little humor paves the way for a warm and relaxed atmosphere.

Avoid triteness. Triteness may be defined as the same old thing in the same old way—boredom results. Be direct, sincere, brisk. Notice how truth and sincerity are integral parts of a speaker or communicator.

Speech of welcome. Know whom you welcome, what he stands for, what he contributes in human attitudes or outlook. Give your welcome an inspirational note. Audiences long to be inspired, uplifted.

Arrange Group Discussions

From simple, easy, and correct speaking experiences, move on to more complex forms.

In planning a group discussion, remember your speaker-listener relationship is "eye meets eye." Do not place your participants so that they cannot see each other easily.

Let each member introduce herself or himself, adding an "identification" line. Be sure each is heard clearly and accurately. Have each member wear a readable name tag.

Provide pencil and paper.

Provide a "visual" board—chalkboard, flannelboard, or storyboard.

Begin on time. Limit speaking time to provide speaking opportunity for each member. Appoint someone to be timekeeper.

If you are a member of the discussion group, do not come to the gathering with a blank mind. Have some information to contribute. This may be knowledge gathered from actual experience or from reading or counsel with others.

Take notes as others speak. Especially jot down names, statistics, or facts hard to recall.

Speak loudly enough for all to hear you. Refer to some remarks previously made by others. Do not contradict statements previously made by others. If you have a contradictory viewpoint, state it simply without offending another.

In the group discussion, you may ask a competent speaker to be leader.

If you are the person asked, know the rules:

As a leader, you are steering the speaker-listener relationship. You are not a speaker yourself.

Keep your group happy. Give each one "equal time." Encourage ease. Make a joke out of an error. Use plenty of good humor. Try to relax anyone not prepared. Come back to him later. Listen with respect. Remember what each one says, as much as possible.

Keep the discussion on the subject. Draw a conclusion now and then to summarize the main contributions.

Call attention to unanswered questions.

Implant a desire in the group to continue further investigation on the matter, whether through personal investigation, reading, counsel with others, or mutual individual discussion.

Call for a break if things are too tense. Let the group "recess" and come back if things get too emotional or if the group is restless from sitting too long.

Invite personal intercommunication during the breaks. These will flow quite naturally, but your referral may encourage more timid members.

Have literature available where unprepared speakers may pick up a thought or two.

Provide a pictorial display, if possible, to stimulate thought.

Begin a literary discussion group. You've finished a reading assignment. Invite your friends to your home for a discussion session. Tell them the purpose of the meeting. Have them give definitions of words: unusual words; colorful words; similes and metaphors they especially liked. Invite others to describe the characters, plot, climax. Ask some to interpret the historical setting of the book, other related factors. Let some give impressions or interpretations gathered during the reading. Develop contributions into a more formal "book review" by a fluent member of the group. From such informal literary discussion groups, a speakers' bureau might be started to speak at meetings throughout the neighborhood.

Learn to combine study with pleasure trips. On long vacation trips, some time might be used as you travel the expressways for reading. At the end of the trip, an informal book discussion would be enjoyable and pleasant.

The world is so full of interesting items, there should be no lack of subjects for observation, investigation, and discussion.

Perhaps no one has ever shown us before that every experience can be a basis for an interesting discussion.

Speaking should be as natural a pastime as eating or recreating, if you will just seize the opportunities within your grasp.

Speech Skill Makes for Citizenship

It may be said you are a good citizen—a useful and vocal citizen—if you are versed in the art of speechmaking. A democracy is made up of people who have ideas, who know how to express them, and who are willing to exchange them with others. Democracy does not begin in Washington or the United Nations, but in every place where children or young people are shown how to speak, when to speak, and why to speak.

Social gatherings are the simplest occasions of which speech is a natural part. As has been observed, social gatherings—teen parties, the breakfast or lunch table, children's parties—all are occasions for improving speech skills. Meals should be occasions in which the mental powers, too, receive nourishment and refreshment. Good conversation has always been a part of good dining. This places responsibilities on each member of the group.

Each member should be prepared to make a contribution to the conversational enjoyment of others; each should have common interests to share with others.

The hosts and hostesses at a formal gathering should have

given careful thought in advance to "directing" conversation along certain paths for the sake of congeniality. Thoughtful hosts will see that each guest is drawn out in conversation, if merely to introduce him to others. Or his opinion may be asked on a certain subject. The same method may be used around a family dining-room table.

Denied Opportunities?

Possibly because you were taught how to read and write much more than you were permitted to argue, discuss, or perform "onstage," silence closed in about you in the schoolroom. Such oral work as you did do was probably in restrained tones. You paid no attention to opening your mouth well when you spoke. Teacher had no time or training to be aware of it or to correct it. Your homework consisted of pages of written exercises. No oral work was ever required! No one thought it important. You went through seven, eight, ten, perhaps twelve years of this type of instruction. No wonder your speech suffered! No one ever suggested that you practice speaking on your own. People thought, and so did you, you could learn only on certain occasions and in certain places, as in school. The fact is, you learn all the time. Every occasion is a learning experience. Since speaking is always part of social affairs, why not create your own special "speech-practice" sessions? If you receive no instruction within your school curriculum, or if you do not provide opportunities for your own instruction, you may emerge, as so many high-school graduates are doing, with a well-trained mind, a physically fit body, but "undeveloped" speech habits. These usually result in speech that is de-energized, unresonant, lazy-lipped and tight-jawed. Naturally, such inexperienced speakers tremble at the thought of speech in public or before an informal group. Careers in speech areas—stage, radio, television, film—never occur to them.

Make Your Own Opportunities

So what happens? You sit and lament? That would be even sadder. Of course not; take yourself in hand. Begin to correct your undesirable habits. Arrange for speech parties within your circle of friends. Organize teen speakers' bureaus. Your local library has information on adult speakers' bureaus that you may study for emulation.

There are many books of simple skits in your library that you may use for "warm-ups" in acting. It is great fun. Begin with simple humorous situations. Then begin to write your own acts. You will find many original thinkers among your group of friends. Work together to write, rehearse, and present original skits before your speech parties' teen-audience.

Use any of the classic plays or musicals to read portions from. Include singing some of the songs, if you wish. Just reading sections of the work aloud will improve your voice and give you confidence.

Talk to children. If you can say and do things that will keep children interested, so that they won't take their eyes off you, then you're a good speaker. Watch teachers of young children on educational television channels. They are experts in attention-holding. These men and women seem to be transformed before your eyes. Their voices, their illustrations, their change of pace, all are designed to hold attention.

Speaking to children will also give you a childlike quality of simplicity. Their reactions are honest. They will give you constructive criticism and suggest what your presentation is lacking. One child, coming from an art museum tour, was asked how he liked the colorful display of pictures.

"They were nice pictures, but they didn't talk . . . not one of them." Children of today's world are experts in the "message" coming through.

Your message must come through, if you are to be effective. Speaking before children will relax you, unfreeze you, and really set you on the path to being a warm, vital, interesting communicator.

Set up shows for children. Get a group of children together in your neighborhood and tell them stories. There are many ways in which you can both use them as a test audience and also be a means of instructing them. Also have the children tell stories. All these activities may be a contribution to your community. During a performance given for the public by a group of teens and children, one boy kept the actors and actresses of the younger set quiet and interested until it was time for them to go onstage. He was "warming up" as an actor, providing occupation for restless little minds, and inspiring the group with purposeful use of time.

Give puppet shows. In our city we have groups of children and teens who have taken instruction in puppetry. They are known as the *Parasol Players.* They make simple puppets, write original scripts or use the old-time favorite fairy tales and classics to entertain children's groups. This entertaining is done in parks or at children's birthday parties. Mothers are always looking for some form of entertainment for the tots, and the *Parasol Players* is the answer. Not only do the young people put on a show, but they assist with the arrangements of the party, help manage the children, and help clean up afterwards.

Other puppet groups entertain at women's clubs and parents' groups. They have solicited the help of parents in making portable stages and wardrobe equipment for their traveling troupe and are quickly and happily learning the thrill of an early start in "show biz."

Not all education takes place in school. Statistics show that more time is spent outside the walls of the classroom than inside. Creative minds will fill that time with creative activity.

Rehearse giving a news report. Choose a story from a newspaper or magazine. Read it out loud to yourself, walking around the room. The important thing is to exercise your vocal cords, to learn to hear spoken words, and to get used to your own voice.

Report a news event, or give a dramatic cutting.

Put the paper down and see how much you can remember and say, in an organized way, without the help of reading. Visualize and talk to an imaginary audience. Go back to the story. Notice how the writer organized it. Read it paragraph by paragraph. After each paragraph, stop and repeat the meaning of what was said there. Summarize the contents into a word or phrase. Jot it down on paper. Do this all through the article. As you finish the last paragraph you will have a complete outline of the development of the information. Now repeat the entire story from the outline. Time yourself. See how long you can talk without reading. You are developing skill in continuity of thought—a most important asset for a speaker. Repeat this process until you can talk easily for from five to seven minutes.

Always remember to observe the rule of *pause:* periods, commas, and the rest. Also, pause for important thoughts or phrases. Articulate correctly.

After so much oral practice, you should now be ready to begin to write!

CHAPTER IV

On Your Mark: You Against Blank Paper

First you write. Look at your thoughts in print. Later you will speak them.

Speechmaking, like writing, demands careful composition. Ideas flow only when concentration is possible; where there is peace and quiet. Surround yourself with books of reference, a dictionary, and plenty of determination that it's going to be a long, hard process. A speaker is a writer who has turned written words into spoken ones.

Begin to build. You achieve structural soundness in your composition by choosing an appropriate subject, adopting a valid approach, dividing your material properly into paragraphs, and adequately developing each one. What do you write about? What do you talk about?

You see an old broken wagon wheel in winter, draped with ice and snow. In summer it becomes a trellis for roses. You begin to see the thinly veiled wonders of life. A great part of life's adventure is the creative response you develop to things most people let go unobserved. Your inner sight can add a new dimension to your day-to-day experience. As a writer-speaker, you need to view the world more closely, respond to it more deeply, and interpret things more creatively. What do you see when you see a rose? What do you hear when you listen to the wind? What do you experience as things happen? Every event has an undiscovered meaning. Every experience is a pressure point directed toward some new and greater unfoldment. Every situation has significance-in-depth leading into a fuller awareness of potentials hidden deep within oneself. What do you see when you see a new superhighway. What do you see in traffic? In the frantic rush of a restless people, or in the affluence and industry of a nation on the move? What do you see in the changing scene through which a morning ride takes you?

As a teen, you are especially proud of your point of view. This is the beginning of original thinking. If your educational background has not contributed to creative thinking within you, develop your own ability. Get new ideas. The earth is crammed with riches to be discovered according to their need. So, also, is life. Nothing in the world is finished today. In every nook and niche of life, from the latest medical breakthrough to the next discovery in outer space, nothing is ever final or fixed or as yet perfectly fulfilled, and in this fact may lie life's greatest meaning. The answer to "What's left for me?" is "Everything!"

Get into action. Michelangelo said that if you draw something, you understand it. Drawing is the mother of learning. Drawing demands acute observation. The drawer must steel himself to see an object or idea as it is, not as he imagines it.

Ask questions endlessly. Answers suggest new questions. Build each question on the framework of the question in the previous answer.

Gather facts with continuity. Logic is like bricklaying. One brick fits onto the one before. Search for the key factor.

Make a storyboard. Write down facts on 3 x 5 cards; then lay them out to see how they fit together. Pin them to the wall if it helps you to see better. Then arrange them in order. Numbers are tools of precision.

Give details. What date? What time? How many? How few? How long ago? How recently? How big? How small?

Adjectives take the place of accurate and definitive information. Do not be satisfied with adjectives alone.

Accept facts with caution. Some information masquerades as

fact, when it is really a collection of false generalizations. A fact is no more than an opinion until it has been subjected to certain rigorous tests:

What is its source? When was the information gathered? To what period of time does it apply? What were the conditions that existed then? What was the method by which the facts were gathered. Is that a biased or a scientific method?

A method of filing information may seem mechanical; it is more than that. Facts can be worked with in a number of ways. A method that files them and keeps them working at the same time is invaluable. A small card system of 3 x 5 cards should be kept containing bits of information. These should be reviewed constantly. Out of this process comes familiarity with the subject matter and gradually an idea as to which facts are the more important.

In defining a problem draw up a tentative definition. Organize and analyze facts relating to the situation. Check each word for meaning. Draw a rectangle around the key words. Try to avoid generalizing adjectives such as *some, many, few, several*. Apply a numbers check. Give dates, times, quantities. Numbers make delineation of problems much clearer to everyone. Check with others for frailty of language. Ask if the words mean to them what they mean to you.

In preparing a problem, sleep on it awhile. Take the problem on vacation. Great thinkers say that in the first working of a hard problem, nothing or little is accomplished. After a rest, long or short, when the work is undertaken anew; ideas begin to pop. Conscious work seems more fruitful because it has been interrupted and the rested mind has more force and freshness to tackle it anew.

After the inspiration, the second period of work begins—the period in which you put in shape the result of the inspiration. Put perspiration into work and the mind soars. Perspiration produces ideas, and ideas are the object of your speech.

Reading is good, but when possible, see for yourself. See where additional research is needed. For the person in search of ideas, there is no substitute for personal investigation.

Slow down when assessing a situation. When is a fact a fact? Investigate who, what, when, why, how, and under what conditions. Time constantly alters the situation. A smart tailor takes the measurements each time he makes a new suit. Facts, like fashions, keep changing with time. Yesterday's facts cannot achieve the solutions to today's objectives. The office boy promoted to a high position still remains an office boy to many. Yet the only measurements that fit him are today's.

Observers do not always understand one seeking personal experience. A bystander remarked of a great botanist:

"Poor man, he just stands and stares at a yellow rose for minutes at a time. It would be better if he had something to do."

The man *was* doing something. He had finished his book and paper work and was now studying the flower with his own eyes, trying to sense its whole complex life. He was *thinking*.

Personal observation does wonders for the creative driving force. Reading is invaluable, but personal experience is indispensable.

Ideas must have sound values. You must have clear ideas of your own, an open mind, and the ability to grasp the ideas of others.

Seriousness is central to growth. Ideas may be taken from various areas: man in society, man creating society, man affected by society.

One attribute that makes you human is your mind. Through it, you perceive the world through a two-way window—from the outside in and from the inside out; with the forward movement of time, you experience changing attitudes toward the external world.

Writing, and eventually speaking, is a process by which you weave together in pleasing texture, color, form, and design a fabric of your thoughts.

Next to *what, how long* is important. Determine how long

your speech must go on; how short dare it be. The length of your speech determines the number and length of parts to fill it. List all subjects you could talk about interestingly, or which are of specific concern.

Specialize. Begin by jotting down on a note pad, as a stream of consciousness, every snatch of thought occurring to you that usefully applies to the subject. Keep pencil and paper beside bed, bath, books. Best thoughts often strike when you are least expecting them. If you are looking for material you will find it. Cull what you can from anything you read. Bend all conversation to the topic on which you wish to write. Put off cronies; drink and dine with interesting people to squeeze ideas out of them. Run all accessible wells dry. Then begin to write.

Opening. The opening must gain immediate attention. By this technique you focus your material, make it important. *This one time is different.* Some things happen hundreds of times, but "this one time it is different." This approach commands attention.

Bait. Make your listeners react. As a writer, your line of thought should move. You are like an acrobat, riding a bicycle on a tightwire. Your audience will gasp when the bicycle wobbles, shriek at a tilt, hold its breath.

Suspense. Everybody expects disaster, and nobody budges from his seat until by almost superhuman skill and effort, the performer reaches the other end of the wire. Then everyone relaxes and says: "Anyone could do it with practice."

One way to entertain people is to give them mental exercise, whether you do it on paper with 5,000 words, or through speaking with 500. If you have a problem, or create people who do, there are always others who will invest time, attention, and sometimes money to see or hear you solve it.

Human Interest. Center on one person in the problem. Thousands of children could starve in Asia, but if you see a child tied in a basement and mistreated, you're much more interested. It's a case of centering on one character or situation. Make it close, understandable, and appealing.

Ideas into Words

Action. Action lines call for short, tense words.

Color. Charles Dickens was an expert. Here is one example:

> COKETOWN
> by Charles Dickens
>
> It was a town of red brick, or of brick that would have been red, if the smoke and ashes had allowed it. It was a town of unnatural red and black like the painted face of a savage.
>
> It was a town of machinery and tall chimneys, out of which undeterminable serpents of smoke trailed themselves for ever and ever, and never got uncoiled. It had a black canal in it, and a river that ran purple with ill-smelling dye, and vast piles of buildings full of windows, where there was rattling and trembling all day long, and where the piston of the steam-engine worked monotonously up and down, like the head of an elephant in a state of melancholy madness.

Notice the color, sound, movement!

> It contained several large streets all very like one another, and many small streets still more like one another, inhabited by people equally like one another, who all went in and out at the same hours, with the same sound.
> —Ibid.

Try to dream up such expressions as: "fossil leaves pressed for time"; "gulls circling the lighthouse awaiting landing instructions"; "waves lowered their heads like bulls and charged the beach"; "patches of fog toured the water front."

Watch advertisements. Advertising is an articulate business. To get ahead, you must prove you are articulate, too.

Avoid clichés—the usual word order. Because they are so familiar, clichés plod past not even heard, let alone seen, in the mind of the audience. Like tickings of clocks, they just don't register. A twist *turns* the meaning.

> "Come to Jamaica—it's *no* place like home!"
> "The cafeteria offers a cuisine second to *any*."
> "Here was a cure, for which there is no known disease."
> "Make hay when the *pun* shines."
> "*Weed* and *reap*."
> "The *wife* you save may be your own."
> "Our carpet covers a multitude of *dins*."

Coining a new label for anything automatically creates something fresh, different, and interesting. "An iron curtain has descended across the continent" (Winston Churchill). "But the New Frontier of which I speak is not a set of promises—it is a set of challenges" (John F. Kennedy).

Buttress your points, whether or not they need it, with apt quotations. Audiences oddly enough admire *borrowers* only slightly less than the authors of brilliant quotes. The luster of their wit rubs off generously on your talk. Many whole successful speeches have been little more than conglomerates of other people's remarks. The Bible is an unique treasure-trove of quotes. Quoting a man also gives the illusion of your familiarity with his entire body of work. This presents proof of your erudition.

An apt saying may be used for an opening, throughout development, or as a closing.

Quotations, or maxims, are sayings of brilliant minds—psychologists, philosophers, poets, thinkers.

> "If we had no faults, we should not take such pleasure in calling attention to other people's."
>
> —La Rochefoucauld

> "We make promises to the extent that we hope—and keep them to the extent that we fear."
>
> —Ibid.

"It is more shameful to distrust our friends than to be deceived by them."
—Ibid.

"The cleverest way for unclever people to act is to turn to their betters for guidance."
—Ibid.

"Knowledge is power."
—Francis Bacon

"States, as great engines, move slowly."
—Ibid.

"The world's a bubble, and the life of a man less than a span."
—Ibid.

"You great sun . . . you rich eye of joy . . . you keep watch, you come, give and share . . ."
—Friedrich Nietzsche

"Homey" sayings endear speakers to their audience. Khrushchev's "ancient" Russian proverbs sound no less authentic for being undoubtedly written to fit the occasion.

"If you don't like the heat, stay out of the kitchen." Harry Truman was a master of homey sayings.

"Her heart was as cold as a depot stove."

Divide your speech into parts, and draw upon a *variety* of different subjects, one for each part. Each subject need have no more in common with its fellows than interests for the particular audience.

"A 'ribbon of relevancy' is better than one long connected whole."

Use watertight compartments like the *Queen Mary*: each an autonomous little speech likely to survive any mishap.

Give it a whirl in the Mixmaster of your mind and experience. Polish it until it sparkles with variety and brevity.

Chip some nuggets from their original settings in literature—mythology, history, fiction, or biography and use them to illustrate what you're talking about. They have a way of making whatever parallel you're drawing seem not only vivid, but valid.

Flavor with humor. A sudden turn in direction, an unexpected ending, earns a laugh.

> The amount of sleep required by the average person is about five minutes more.
> Statement: Am without friends or funds. Answer: Make friends.

Repeating the same word or phrase gives emphasis:

> Fact, fact, fact, everywhere in the material;
> fact, fact, fact, everywhere in the immaterial.

Vitalized statistics can enliven a speech when translated into word pictures that the audience can look and wonder at. The more picturesque they are, the less their accuracy seems to be questioned. Example: "Do you have any idea how large the national debt really is? It could carpet this state wall-to-wall!"

Visual aids make what is heard seem better than it is. Accompany your remarks with interesting visual aids (not dreary charts or graphs) for your listeners to look at as they listen. A visual aid is a superb camouflage—when an audience is looking at one, it's not looking at you. This is an advantage, a pleasant shift in vision.

The ultimate sophistication of the visual aid in the camouflage department is the slide or movie talk, which permits a speech to be delivered in darkness with speaker (and nervousness) invisible. The single most memorable element in many a successful speech has been a visual aid.

Visual and audio aids become doubly effective when turned

into demonstrations. Here the speaker uses props either to make a dramatic comparison or to make something happen—or both. The technique used in TV commercials is a white glove on a greasy scalp; hair spray so clear you can't see it when it's sprayed on a mirror, etc.

The most helpful audio aids, any speaker in the act of speaking will agree, are an audience's applause and (when appropriate) its laughter. Often a way to create the climate for both is with sound effects, which at least never fail to sharpen a point.

Writing for spoken delivery should be simple; comprehensible at the 12-year-old level. Muddiness of sense and syntax show up as muddy to listeners. Rewrite and retest until you get an all-clear signal.

Your sentences must flow. A good piece of writing moves along like a well-oiled machine. There are no sudden stops and starts, no sputtering, no unevenness. Each thought flows from the one preceding it and into the one following it. Within each paragraph, the sentences repeat the same pattern, following one another easily, in a clearly connected way, toward the central idea. The professional calls this kind of smoothness *continuity*. Achieving it is not difficult. It is done with words and phrases strategically placed to form links in a chain of thoughts and ideas.

Continuity in sentences will lead to continuity in paragraphs. The last sentence of the beginning paragraph is picked up and carried forward by the first sentence of the middle paragraph. However, the words are changed for the sake of variety. Or they may be repeated for the sake of emphasis.

Use fables. Audiences, like children, like fables. Set a scene in the forest, stock it with furred or feathered friends, and tell a tale. Don't worry if the plot merely points up a platitude. Fables are like animal crackers: shape enchances content.

People never fail to accept a fable's denouement as wisdom; its moral as wit.

Keep an idea box. Writers keep idea boxes. Drop into it quotations cut out from Sunday editions of newspapers, human interest stories that crowd every column, unusual pictures, unique reports; reliable statistics, catchy titles, phrases, opening thoughts, good concluding expressions. File them neatly, so as to be able to find what you want when you want it. If exact quotes are used, credit must be given to the writer or the publication. However, the idea may stimulate a new thought for you so you can dress up the original piece of information in new clothes. You are on your way to winning the battle of black ink against white paper.

Keep a notebook. Some writers get thoughts at unlikely moments. They grab the nearest piece of paper, old envelope, shopping bag, or newspaper to record a thought that has just struck them. Rather than this haphazard practice, always carry a notebook. Beginnings will be very crude, but at least will be a beginning. More refining and polishing will help. At least from your bad efforts you can pick out the good ones.

Write, then cut. The more a speech is cut, the better it is. Cut anything that doesn't clearly state meaning, illustrate it, or amuse. The best sentence is a simple declarative. Cut transitions, step as directly as possible from part to part. Cut generalizations and abstractions.

Encapsulated Summings-Up

Whenever a speaker encapsulates a whole kettle of fish in a kindergarten-simple summing-up, he can't help but seem in command of his material and himself. Minor miracles of miniaturization are usually little more than gross over-simplifications concealed by the neatness of their package. For instance:

"Mind the three p's of cosmetics: product, promise, profit."
"The only thing we have to fear is fear itself."
"Call to arms! may ennoble disagreeable chores. Make everyone want to run to get into the act!"
"The job ahead isn't easy."

"A lot of people are going to get killed."
"Everyone will have to pitch in."
"I have nothing to offer you but blood, toil, tears, and sweat."

People expect a speaker to approach the microphone fearlessly. The least smell of fear may be fatal. Fear ranges from the parent confronted with addressing the P.T.A. on elementary school problems to the apparently polished politician outwardly as cool as his carnation, but inwardly (and there are many) sore afraid. The technique works whether you have anything to say or not.

The secret of a good speaker is to keep the audience so absorbed, diverted, preoccupied, or entertained that it doesn't have a chance to notice the speaker's terror.

People are the animals most capable of boring each other simply because they're the only ones that talk. No kind of talking can have a higher-caliber bore than public talking. Everyone has sat through his share of speeches that have made him wish that not freedom *of,* but freedom *from* speech had been included in the Bill of Rights. While authorities itemize all kinds of speeches, there are indeed but two kinds: boring and nonboring.

Nobody thinks the same of a speaker *after* a talk as *before.* Opinion is worse or better, according to the kind of speech he gives. Conventional speakers make the error of conceiving of a speech as the decline and fall of the Roman Empire with an Aristotelian beginning, a middle, and (only at last) an end. But they seem rarely able to come up with enough speechworthy material to sustain interest through an entire speech.

A final test of writing: Is it speechworthy? Think of the audience as it grows bored, free to focus its attention more upon speaker than speech, and to seize upon anything interesting to occupy its mind . . . than which there's no tenant so fascinating as a speaker's nervousness. The nervous speaker, sensing this, simply produces still more nervous symptoms for his audience to observe.

Writing and speaking call for hard work. But there's glory

in it. No small amount of time and effort goes into a creation All of it is hard work. When it's over, you forget the hard work. An artist commented, after laboring through hours of physical hardship to paint a picture, "The pain stops; the beauty goes on."

Imitate models. Painters learn to paint by studying models. Speakers learn to speak by writing and studying models of composition, such as Lincoln's Gettysburg Address. To this day, no one knows precisely when or how this was written. Few contemporaries of Lincoln could agree on whether he read it from a paper or spoke from memory, whether there was applause, or whether he was even heard.

There is the popular notion that he wrote the speech on the train that took him to Gettysburg. This legend is well fostered by many highly placed "witnesses" who claimed they rode in his private compartment. If all reports are to be believed, the compartment must have been so jam-packed that poor Mr. Lincoln was lucky to get a seat.

"Eyewitnesses" say Lincoln propped his stove-pipe hat on his knees, using the top as a desk, and wrote the speech on a slip of paper. Some say he used brown wrapping paper.

One account has it that he borrowed the pencil from Andrew Carnegie. There is no evidence that Carnegie was even on the train. It is well authenticated that he wrote the first part of the speech before he left the White House, the second part after he arrived in Gettysburg. If he wrote anything on the train, it apparently wasn't the great speech. Library of Congress records contain fascinating nuggets about the speech. He copied the original one for a friend and three times to be auctioned off for charity. A further mystery is that no two copies read precisely the same, and none agrees precisely with what observers reported he said at Gettysburg.

Was the speech poorly received? Historians report that it fell on the crowd like "A wet blanket." (This popular expression goes that far back.)

It is perhaps true that Lincoln himself was disappointed in the speech, but he could not have worried for long. In the next few days, at least twenty of the nation's leading dailies and weeklies headlined the speech as a masterpiece of eloquence.

Could Lincoln be heard? Many say his voice was too high and weak to carry. Others say his voice was loud and clear, and many more heard him than heard Edward Everett.

A favorite mystery about the address is the phrase "government of the people, by the people, for the people." There is scarcely any Lincoln quotation more familiar than this. But curiously enough, it is perhaps the only part of the Gettysburg Address he did not create. The phrase had been used, with slight variations, by many speakers and writers before Lincoln, most notably by Thomas Cooper in 1795, John Adams in 1798, John Marshall in 1819, Daniel Webster in 1830, and by Theodore Parker on three different occasions in 1850, 1854, and 1858.

Did Lincoln know that he was "quoting?" There is reason to believe that he had read it and checked it in a pamphlet of a sermon by Parker. Possibly it came back to him when he was grasping for a strong finish to his speech. (He admitted he was having trouble with the finish.)

But it's an unimportant mystery. The point is that it was Lincoln—not Parker, Webster, Adams, or anyone else—who made it the everlasting rallying-cry of democracy.

As a speech student, analyze the composition—the beginning, middle, and end.

It is a masterful piece of work. Its greatest merit, however, lay in the sincerity and eloquence of the delivery.

Today's models. The late Reverend Martin Luther King Jr. was a modern artist in the craft of speechmaking. In his now-famous "I Have a Dream" speech, he used a title to become a recurring theme throughout an appealing composition. A theme may be considered a "ribbon of relevancy" to tie varieties of thoughts into a compact package. A theme creates unity at the same time that the repetition of it creates emphasis.

Doctor King relied heavily on scriptural quotations for source material. He borrowed frequently, too, from historical quotations, and inserted extracts of patriotic songs and hymns. He combined these thoughts with his own to weave a new artistic composition. He built to a climax and, with fire and fervor, looked to the future for improvement of conditions, appealing to help from Almighty God in his closing statement.

The thoughts of Doctor King were powerful, but teens of today can remember, too, the living power of his voice and the dynamism of his delivery.

Imitate these as you set about your career of speechmaking.

The late President John F. Kennedy was a friend of youth. He was a master debater and orator. His speeches were fresh, alive, timely. You may remember hearing some of them in his own living voice. You may hear him on record at your public library. His last proclamation was one of thanksgiving written and delivered in the fateful November, 1963.

Through John F. Kennedy's speeches, his spirit lives on. A man never dies as long as he can be read, or better, "heard." Kennedy's speeches were usually prepared in rough draft, by a White House aide. The revising and rewriting was always done by President Kennedy himself. Into the thoughts and words he impressed his own thought and style. When his last speech appeared in the press, the man who prepared it for his people was dead. The people, in too great a state of shock and grief to remember other blessings, did not hear it.

In days of calmer emotions, it can be retrieved from oblivion. The message will be timely today as it was yesterday.

President Kennedy usually used a dash of historical perspective for an opening. Can you remember his vibrant, rich voice; his impassioned vigor; his balanced, rhythmic sentences?

Following the opening, the next few paragraphs detail the history of Thanksgiving since the time of the Pilgrims.

The JFK style is apparent in the closing paragraph. In it he brings his listener "over the river and through the woods" to the scene of today's American life. Notice his use of alliteration in phrases such as "our power has grown; so has our peril." He concluded with a plea for help from on high and united action from a united America. It was the last presidential speech to bear the signature: *John F. Kennedy.*

CHAPTER V

Get Set: You Against the Written Page

Rehearsal is the next step in preparing your career as a speechmaker. Examine the word *rehearsal* to see that it means to *re-hear*. Through repeating the words many times; through re-hearing yourself speak, your tongue gains a familiarity with the syllables, your ear with the sounds as your mind absorbs the ideas. Rehearsal should always be done aloud. You may memorize silently; but your voice must be heard if you are to re-hear yourself. You may walk around the room and listen to yourself; you may ask someone else to listen to you, or you may use a tape recorder.

As a speaker, remembering will be part of your business. Luckily, you can greatly increase—and easily—the amount and accuracy of what you remember.

Remembering is a necessary function that enables you to cope successfully with life. The excuse, "I just can't remember," is sheer nonsense.

Remembering is essential to success in any walk of life. It is the power by which the past is bound to the present; the present to the future. Remembering keeps your mental machinery active. If there is little remembering, there cannot be much thinking. The better you remember, the more efficiently will your work be done.

Speech skills especially require the art of remembering. Whether you think so or not, remembering is important in decision-making and in other unthought-of areas, such as social manners and in understanding other people.

In reading, test your ability to remember. Can you recall half of what you read, more than half, the entire unit? This will give you some indication of your power of recall—of remembering.

Remembering is a means of testing mental activity. In order to remember a fact, you must *want* to remember it. You must give the fact active attention at the time of hearing it. You must look at the fact, listen to it, talk about it and think about it at the time it enters your mind.

Some things can be learned only be rote; others can be learned only by rote plus understanding. In memorizing speeches, both are necessary. The more associations a thing has, the more meaning it will have. If you are trying to memorize, try also to get the meaning—to understand what you are saying. Check the meaning of words. Once this is done, remembering the idea requires little effort.

Millions of school children pledge allegiance to the flag. In order for the pledge to mean anything, all the words must be understood. How can a child understand the words "allegiance" or "indivisible" or "justice for all"? He has no concepts of these words. He is merely repeating sounds.

The same is true of prayers, so-called, that exceed his limit of comprehension. It is no wonder, then, he is jumbling phrases like "Halloween Thy name." He *does* have a concept of Halloween. Another young New Yorker whispered: "Lead us not into Penn Station."

We laugh at children's misunderstandings, at the same time as we force them into rote memorization of words far beyond their years. It is no wonder teachers find that students never bother to look up the meanings of words. Rote learning has been the only kind they have known.

Unless you understand the meaning of words, you are a rote learner and an ineffective and mechanical speaker.

Inverted order will give you trouble, possibly, in memory work. "Ray serene" will be harder to memorize than "serene ray." To be able to remember some fact about 1914, you will need a broader knowledge of 1914 than the mere fact upon which you are concentrating. Much of your learning is not preceded or surrounded by sufficient background learning. This is the area in which reading and travel can be of help. The more associations you have, the more meaning you will get from ideas.

Never be content with learning the form and not the content. This will be one of the points on which a listener, or your speech judge, will evaluate you—do you understand the subject?

If you have written a speech and wish to memorize it for presentation, involve yourself in it. Be interested in it. Know enough about it for it to be real to you. Integrity, truthfulness, sincerity will shine out. One easily remembers what is a part of oneself.

As in writing the speech be sure to have the right environment for studying it. Get away from distractions. Avoid the telephone. No radio, TV, or record player. No noise from inside or outside.

Be awake. You are wasting your time if you are not alert. Your mind will not function.

Say the first sentence out loud. Say it again. Listen to the words. Verbalizing strengthens the motor and mechanical operations for memory. For the acquisition of information, sight and hearing are important senses. Better learning takes place when the senses reinforce each other.

Say it again. Keep repeating. Add a new phrase. Repeat it several times. Now say the whole sentence. Continue this way until you have *said* and *heard yourself say* three or four sentences. Walk around as you do this. Talk out loud. Repeat this process until you begin to tire.

When you flag, break off and do something else for a little while. Come back. Begin again.

Try ten minutes at a time to begin. Lengthen the time as you develop endurance in memory work.

Use a tape recorder to record what you have said. Begin again.

Put it away and do something else. After a time, come back and begin again. You will be surprised how much you remember. Go over the weak spots. Repeat many times any word or phrase that seems "stubborn." Begin to feel natural and let movements, or gestures, accompany the words.

Come back again later. Even if it is the next day, keep harping, repeating, repeating. Record the whole thing on tape and let it play as you do other chores: make the bed, arrange your hair, wash the dishes, clean the car. The repetition is the most important element, once the pattern in words has been set. You will be surprised at the manner in which your mind will look forward to what is coming next. You will marvel at your own ability to use your memory.

Many speech tournaments call for word-for-word memorization of a speech.

Stage work requires that you know the script *verbatim*. You can imagine what would happen in a theatre if each character ad-libbed. For set productions, every act hinges on word cues. As a cue is spoken, an action occurs. If the word is missed, everything falls apart. Hence, the words must be in the same order—the *exact* order. Memory is very necessary to actors and actresses.

Unless words are accurately memorized, words of an original speaker are distorted. Word distortion may cause meaning distortion. It is necessary to have a written script of every important speech for purposes of release. Speakers on television, who do not have time to write or memorize speeches, depend on the TelePrompTer, a device that spins off the words as the speaker reads them. Watch a television speaker, and especially the position and movements of his eyes. They will be slightly raised and shift from right to left. You can recognize the fact that he is reading from a TelePrompTer.

In learning a formal speech, the outline should be studied

most thoroughly until its themes and logic become crystal clear. First step is to identify the theme and understand it clearly. Memorized speeches are important because they are particularly eloquent and provide just the needed emphasis; furthermore, you may wish to use quotations, and these must be repeated accurately.

One speaker who began to memorize found that towards the end he could memorize ten times as fast as at the beginning. It is said that in a second play it is much easier to learn lines than in the first.

In learning long pieces, spacing and review are of utmost importance. The poorer the organization of the speech, the harder it is to understand and to remember. Since memory results from learning, and learning is a skill, improvement in learning and therefore, in remembering, can be achieved. As learning becomes more significant and more rapid, the stored wealth of memory, based on such learning, can be trained to function more efficiently, and, in certain cases, the extent of improvement can be very great. Some people possess more aptitude and can progress more rapidly than others. But anyone who gives care to his methods of learning can improve his memory.

As memory is part of the mechanism of adjusting to life, it can be expected that particular memories will be frequently changed by the redefinitions that come with a person's experience and with the new patterns that develop from his new goals and new information. The memory is a dynamic organization of ideas by which the individual lives and interprets his environment. It is not, as some have thought, merely a quantity of inert thoughts left over from the past.

Forgetting begins slowly, then speeds up with the passage of time. The best time to review is, therefore, soon after learning has taken place. Some record in diaries important happenings that have occurred during the day.

If you can spend two hours mastering a unit of a subject, you would do well not to put in the two hours at one sitting because fatigue would set in and attention would slacken. It would be better to work no more than an hour. Spaced half hours would be even better and not so wearing.

Sleeping on it. Sleep "that knits up the ravell'd sleave of care" will not knit up your raveled memories, but it is a good idea to run through a passage you wish to memorize just before going to sleep. This will often "fix" the passage in your mind.

Use some such memory device as:

rhymes	pigeonholing
numbering	translation
alphabetical order	paired associates
phrases	association chains
acrostics	

Some people sort items into an alphabetical list. For instance, if a housewife wanted to remember bananas, tea, and cereal as her shopping needs, she would rearrange the items in alphabetical order and then say to herself: *b, c, t.* Later, as she shops, she immediately remembers what she wants.

If she wished to stop at the post office after shopping, she would mentally note: "Supermarket, Post Office." "S-P." These simple methods work and are easy to manage. Try them.

Divide and Conquer. If there is something especially long you must remember, divide it into digestible parts. If you were going to eat a pie, you would not try to do it all at one bite or one sitting. You would cut a piece first. You would further subdivide the piece into manageable bites. Be as kind to your mental powers as to your physical powers. If you wish to memorize eight lines, begin with the first line. Then break the first line down into phrases. Say the first phrase over until you can do so from memory. Then work on the second phrase. Then join them. Continue. If you become tired, go away and do something else. Then return to see if you can repeat the section you have studied.

If you were to memorize a number like this:

$$2368309762406385$$

you might find it difficult. However, this might be possible:

$$236 \quad 830 \quad 976 \quad 240 \quad 6385$$

You have divided to conquer. The same effect as the space is achieved by a comma. The purpose of punctuation is to pause for thought—hence for understanding.

Don't be a foolish teen who says: "But I just can't remember. Honest, you don't know how bad my memory is. Why, I just never could remember."

In order to remember:

Use grouping and rhythm—even beat out the rhythm of the words as you say them aloud.
Be confident you can remember.
Visualize—see it in your mind's eye.
Try to remember and recall—concentrate.
Memorize by meanings rather than by sounds.
Study a bit at a time; then put the whole together.
Keep what you want to remember the center of your attention—avoid distraction while memorizing.
Associate the new knowledge with former knowledge.

The greatest advantage of being proficient in speaking skills is that you become a better student. It is virtually impossible to be an accomplished student of speech and be a failure as a student. Speaking, like study, is an *active* process.

Your memory is active at all times. As you perform some physical activity, suddenly an "association" of thoughts pops into your consciousness. Two mental elements are moving together to make a whole new concept. This is the beginning of the process of creativity. Little children seem to remember this way. They cannot summarize. When returning from school, Mother says:

"Johnny, what did you do in school today?"

This is too much of a mental jolt to Johnny. He answers, truthfully or not:

"Nothing."

But as Johnny plays with his toys or is put to bed, he will be able to recall fantastic details through his power of association—as what he is doing is linked with something he did somewhere else.

Getting the meaning is important for remembering. Little children do not get meaning. This comes only with the use of reason. But teens should get meaning and be able to remember.

Ask questions! You cannot remember things you did not understand. If there is a missing link in the chain of related facts, you will have to stop and get the fact. This is the place to make an inquiry, ask a question, get direction. It is as important as the instruction period. Students who never ask questions are possibly students who are missing links of meaning, but do not admit it. If you cannot get the answer on the spot, then go to the nearest library and look it up, or ask one of your companions who may have understood the point. Failures in school, and hence dropouts, may be the result of many, many bits of information not understood all along the line of education from kindergarten up. The final accumulation of missing information causes discouragement that is too great to bear.

Children ask questions. They are sincere and honest about acquiring knowledge. The questions are many and constant. Their incessant, and at times, embarrassing, questions round out their conceptions and lead them to broader ideas that can do better work than a minimum of meager facts.

What happens to teens in class? Are they honest enough to ask questions? Many teachers will admit failure in imparting knowledge is due to the fact that high-school students do not "communicate" in class. They neither ask questions nor offer responses. Perhaps this is the fault of the educational system and not the fault of the teens. The situation, too, may be the result of a system that has always required information to be recorded in writing, not through oral channels.

Some teachers resort to the written word for an indication of the amount of knowledge students have gained. This is time-consuming and laborious, both for the student writing and for the teacher checking. But this will be the status quo until the era of oral communication in the educational process.

Never underestimate your power! Your memory is an agile faculty and will serve you well, if you will let it. It is your duty to train and develop it. One advantage of memory is convenience. Your brain has great computer ability. It will serve you with a fact much more quickly and accurately than you could find it by shuffling through piles and pages of notes.

Do not be misled by the "ingenious" memory of others. They followed the same course in developing their skills.

Arturo Toscanini, for example, could conduct symphonies without the aid of written scores. General George C. Marshall could discuss from memory almost every event of World War II; he organized and arranged facts in his mind as he did soldiers on the field. Organization and repetition are always the keys.

Napoleon is said to have remembered thousands of his soldiers' names.

Motivation can work wonders. In a classroom a certain boy told his teacher that Lincoln's Birthday would come on a Thursday. His teacher praised him for this observation. Delighted, he turned to the calendar for further study. He became a wonder as he amazed people with day-and-date stunts, although he never became generally educated.

It's not always the most gifted who excels. The old Aesop fable of the hare and the tortoise is still true. The one who plods along painstakingly each day can far outrun those with greater skill who sit down to rest.

Demosthenes, the famous Greek orator, had a lisp. But he went to the seashore and filled his mouth with pebbles and practiced until he could speak plainly with a mouthful of stones! Above the roaring of the waves at the Grecian beach, he taught himself to speak clearly and with volume. Having overcome his handicap through motivation and determination, he could return to the Greek Forum to take his place with his gifted associates.

Toscanini memorized musical scores because he had poor eyesight; if he was to be a conductor he had to memorize music because he could not read it while conducting. A blind lawyer memorized legal details for similar reasons.

Charles Kettering, the inventor of the self-starter on motors, also suffered from poor eyesight. He got his room companion to read to him, while he listened and memorized the facts.

It may be safe to say that all persons who have developed remarkable memories have done so because of a driving need or desire. Napoleon remembered vast arrays of facts to serve his ambition.

Many boys who do poorly in school nevertheless possess an extensive knowledge of baseball. The difference between Joe's knowledge of baseball and his command of spelling is explained by the fact that he is interested in baseball, but is not interested in spelling, and also by the fact that his study of baseball is voluntary, whereas spelling is imposed upon him.

Some merit may also lie in the fact that baseball is a physical activity and more pleasant to Joe, whereas spelling is routine and mechanized. Much needs to be done still in the area of equating spelling with baseball as far as being a pleasurable exercise. The fact of the matter is, *Joe can memorize.*

Emotion and memory. Strong emotion can do many things to the personality. It can seriously affect the memory.

It is told of Henry Clay that he wished to make a brief statement in the Senate on a point under discussion. He asked a friend to nudge him after five minutes. The friend nudged. He nudged again, but Clay's concentration was so intense, the emotion so high, that even when the friend took a pin and pierced his skin, Clay did not notice it.

Memory, or attention and learning, cannot operate under deep-seated anxieties. Many students with excellent I.Q.'s do not learn, held back by mental strain and stress. Mental activity is diverted into other channels; none is left for learning.

Love is a powerful emotion. It can cause you to remember or forget. Anger is another. An angry driver is apt to be thinking about a traffic quarrel instead of remembering to watch the road.

A speaker who has had no previous experience before a group or audience is emotionally paralyzed if he attempts to speak. However, there is no need for you to be afraid if you follow the simple rules of preparation and practice.

Get a coach! If you really want to learn to do something, get a coach. Coaches know in advance what mistakes a person is likely to make and can often ward off these mistakes. He'll give you a workout; he'll demand that you follow his advice. With these helps, you're sure to try—and probably win!

Mark Twain, who had difficulty remembering his lectures, thought up the device of drawing series of pictures on a piece of paper to illustrate the points of his lecture. This proved to be his best memory aid. Many years later, he could use his pictures to recall the thoughts he wished to express.

A diagram serves several purposes. It helps you to clarify certain facts by simplifying them and arranging them logically. It makes you want to be sure about understanding your facts since you must do so in order to draw the diagram; you absorb the information in more than one way, thus reinforcing your memory; you heighten your interest in the subject through personal involvement, doing something creative with the facts.

Study by phrases. People who study one word at a time tend to lose track of the thought because it takes them so long to get through the sentence. But if you read by phrases, you are able to grasp more ideas because you are now thinking in thought patterns.

A judicious use of pen or pencil as you read a book is a valuable study technique.

Recitation. Recite as student and as your own teacher. Rate yourself. Recitation serves to let the learner know when his task is completed. It saves time and effort because it reveals just where more study is required. It promotes faster learning because it is a more active process than listening or reading. Recitation leads to the detection and correction of mistakes.

Once the printed words are impressed in your memory you are ready for the next step. Polish your voice. The best speakers pause often. In the example below, slashes (/) indicate pauses. Words that should be emphasized (spoken with more force) are underscored. Good speakers strive for variety; loud and soft; use changes in facial expression, gestures, and position.

A Defense of Capital Punishment
by Daniel Webster

The secret which the murderer possesses / soon comes to possess him,/ and like the evil spirit of which we read,/ it overcomes him,/ and leads him wheresoever it will./ (Longer pause)
He feels it beating at his heart,/ rising to his throat,/ demanding disclosure./ He thinks the whole world / sees it in his face,/ reads it in his eyes,/ and almost hears its workings / in the very silence of his thoughts. (Soften voice to get *silence* effect; lower volume)
(Longer pause)
It has become his master. (Louder) It betrays his discretion. (Keep building louder) / It conquers his prudence./ (Soften and pause) (Pick up speed) When suspicions from without begin to embarrass him (hold pitch) and the net of circumstances to entangle him,/ the fatal secret struggles with still greater violence / to burst forth./ (Heighten volume)
(Long pause)

The crime must be confessed. (Soften and slow down. Pause) There is <u>no</u> refuge from confession / but <u>suicide</u>,/ and (slow, soft) <u>suicide</u> is <u>confession</u>.

Gestures. As you feel the words, gestures come naturally. Gestures are simply emotions felt through physical action. For example, as you say "he feels it beating at his heart," your hand may automatically reach toward your heart; as you continue, "rise to his throat," you may feel an urge to continue the gesture in that direction. The best rule for using gestures is to let them flow naturally. Too much action distracts from the words; the right amount lends emphasis and relieves monotony. The speaker himself will decide where and when to use gestures—meaningful movements. When used properly, they add to the effectiveness of delivery.

The markings used in the above example may be necessary for a beginner in interpretation. However, as you acquire skill and experience in speaking, you will be able to do this easily for yourself. Once you have heard good speakers and heard them often, you will "hear" interpretation as you read a printed selection to yourself. You will know how it it will sound aloud.

Record your final achievement on tape, switching from the role of speaker to listener. You hear with your own ears what you really sound like. Just as important, you learn what the speech itself really sounds like. Sentences, phrases, even words that look pretty on paper may be awkward, inappropriate, or even dull when heard aloud. A speech auditioned on tape can be "fixed" until it sounds right.

Your own personal performance will be sharpened, too. Too much monotone? Let your voice rise and fall in the appropriate places on the next try. Talking too fast or too slow, slurring or "eating" your words, or failing to punch home key words? Keep taping it over and over until you get it right. Then go out, give your speech, and please your audience.

A chance to hear yourself is more enlightening than a thousand exhortations from a director.

Ask for criticism. John Barrymore once consoled a young actress who was in tears over critics' reviews.

"It's easy for you to talk," sighed the beginner. "The critics' raves made you a star."

"Yes, I know," said Barrymore. "Only after their earlier notices forced me to become a good actor."

So criticism helps. Instead of being hurt, use it for a stepping stone to improvement. Remember, not all criticism is destructive.

After some speeches, you will have a feeling of great satisfaction. Others will leave you with a feeling that you need to rewrite or rehearse certain areas. But before you know it, you may find yourself too "popular" to stop.

Robert Benchley says of his writing career: "It took fifteen years to discover I had no talent for writing, but I couldn't give it up because by that time I was too famous."

Listening opportunities. Your public library contains many records of all types of literature. Listen to the reading of poetry, the narration of prose. Obtain records of documentary speeches. In these you are able to study the composition and structure of sentences, as well as listen to the vibrating voice of the speaker. Many of these documentaries are live recordings of public figures, prominent in your contemporary life. Listen to them and see how the speech reveals the character.

The ability to imitate a particular kind of speech or to pick up a dialect are other skills that can be acquired by listening to records.

Listen to the voices of actors and actresses. This is a delightful pastime, as well as good ear training. Listen to others speak, then record the same selection on the tape recorder yourself. Rerun the most climactic scene several times.

Record your own voice and the voices of your friends. You can spend an enjoyable session noting the good qualities of each and possible areas of improvement.

For listening exercise, you will need access to a record player, a tape recorder, and a supply of speech records, both for articulation exercises and for practice in acting extracts of plays.

As in your personal book collection, begin also a collection of tapes and records of nonbook materials. If possible, get sound tracks of the actual performances of professionals in order to get the life and fire of the on-the-spot communication miracle—the real voices, the laughter, the sound effects and music, the reaction of the audience, the applause. If this is not possible, recordings are available from many university speech labs.

Begin your collection slowly. Start with one good tape, then add another. But begin your listening program. As you listen, certain nerve paths will be cut into your "hearing mechanism," and you will begin to understand much more clearly how to speak yourself. This is the principle on which small children are able to repeat television commercials at an early age—by rote.

Hear an entire play right through. Let your imagination create the scenes. Your memory will recreate them if you have seen a live production onstage. Enjoy the depth and beauty of the voices. Respond to the changes in pitch and speed. Rise to the emotional climaxes. Allow your ear full play in giving you as theatrical an experience as possible.

Then listen to a section of the play with the script in hand.

Speechmaking is a very important study if you expect to become an actor or actress, amateur or professional.

All the speaking experiences you have had from childhood on will be of the greatest importance to you. If you have built good speech habits—a desire to speak and entertain others, clear and precise diction, pleasant vocal quality—you should have a good chance to succeed.

Speech is only one part of acting, but it is the most direct means of human communication and hence of communication from the stage. But speech on the stage is speech that must grow. It must grow in sharpness and size, as well as in beauty and power. At the same time it is controlled, it must be relaxed; it must be exact, yet free. Its offstage naturalness must be disciplined by training, so that when it is enlarged onstage, it sounds as natural as possible. On the stage, you achieve technical mastery of speech production. Working towards a goal of speaking onstage will give you the motivation you need to accomplish this ability.

You will have to work, but the work will be pleasant and enjoyable. Just as dancers and musicians go through warming-up exercises to get good muscle tone, actors and actresses do the same. Speech exercises warm up the facial muscles, the vocal tract, the breath supply. You come alive as you go through the syllable-by-syllable drills.

Speech exercises also give you practice in flexibility and power. These you will need for projection. Every actor or actress will spend time reading aloud in rehearsal sessions in order to get the feel of the words, the thought sequences, the nuances of meaning. Students who have learned the art of reading aloud early in life will have an advantage over those who have not worked in speech training. In the early years, the muscles are very pliable; children are very uninhibited and free in movement.

Stage performance of speech gives it an added dimension of glory not appreciated in day-to-day communication. Yet the same rules govern each—an open jaw, good articulation practices, sufficient breath supply, enthusiasm, and a vital personality.

Attend live theatre as often as you can. Watch the oral work of the people onstage—the mouth movements of the speakers. Suddenly the role of these movements in shaping the sounds of speech becomes clear. The agility of tongue, lip, and jaw movements, if the actor's speech is well articulated, should be most instructive for you.

While live theatre is the best place to study live voice production, you may have the same experience by watching television. Turn off the sound, now and then, and be conscious only of the oral movements of those on the screen.

Listen to good spoken records for articulation, pausing, inflection, and interpretation, also for voice improvement.

Argumentation may be considered the field and function of the defense attorney or the political or public official. Argumentation is closely allied to public speaking; it is debate, or two contesting and opposing points of view.

Argument amounts to little without the addition of the life-giving element of persuasion. A classic example is the letter written by Agrippina, mother of Nero, the cruel and powerful emperor, pleading for her own life when he had condemned her to death. Another is that of the Roman Seneca to his friend Lucullus denouncing the treatment of slaves and urging a return to the human ways of the old Romans.

Exposition, explaining your point of view, may lead to persuasion or even agreement with your own views. Edmund Burke and his writing and speeches before Parliament, demanding more justice in Britain's handling of the American colonies, are a shining example of a man who thought for himself and tried to convince others of the rightness of his thinking.

Rehearsal range. You are giving yourself practice in various forms of writing and speaking. You are dealing with sophisticated topics and unsophisticated ones, thus giving your voice and memory a wide span of development. Flexibility and adaptability should be your desired outcome.

If you are reading to or telling children the story of the Three Bears, change your voice to imitate Father Bear, Mother Bear, and Baby Bear. This will not take much imagination. Children are your best test as an audience. By talking to children you develop simplicity, humility, and directness. Children naturally react freely. They quickly show their feelings. The person must successfully hold their attention and therefore be the one who makes good use of action stories, picture words, and gestures.

Speech books, hundreds of which are available, too, on your library shelves, will give charts by which you may evaluate your performance. Points cover voice, articulation, subject matter, delivery, and fine points of improvement you will want to remember as you prepare for the big moment to come.

Evaluation enables you to move forward. Your efforts will not be repetitious if you know what to correct and how.

With your subject matter well worked out, with plenty of rehearsal and practice sessions, you will feel a confidence and eager anticipation to meet your actual speaking situation.

CHAPTER VI

Go! You Before Your Audience

You are now about to face the most wonderful group of people you have ever met—your audience. If, up to this point, you have never spoken in public before a large group, a treat lies in store for you. You will appear before an assembly of people who are waiting for one person in the world—*you!* The thrill you will experience as they see you, hear you, and react to you is nothing short of magic. For this golden moment you have labored long and hard. You have written your speech with their interests in mind. You have worked into it all the artistic skill of which you have been capable. You have rehearsed it and polished it. You have asked for critics to help you improve it. You have been your own critic by listening to and improving your style on a tape recorder. You are prepared to meet your audience.

In the first section of this book, you thought about *you!* You considered the inner you more than the outer. You asked yourself the question, "Why do I think it all happens on the outside?" That was the beginning of your thinking about your audience. Your audience will see the *inner you* as you address them in the words you have prepared for them. Those words should be words of faith, of hope, and of love. From these great sources, your audience will gain new strength and courage. For this they give you time, attention, and interest.

From the process of research you have carried on, you may bring new or additional information to your listeners. In this then, you act as a *conveyer of truth.* As the earth revolves each day, more and more research reveals more and more depths of truth in more and more areas. No one individual has the time or the access to all knowledge. It is through your role as a speaker that you may present your audience with one more bit of information.

In impressing a listener, you do not necessarily add to his fund of information. You do select certain items on which your audience has some knowledge, you ask for reconsideration, rethinking of an important point.

To impress people, you need to make the problem a personal one to them. You have some light to shed on a dark area of their concern; you have some advice to give in a course that calls for direction. You help them to realize the importance of the point under consideration: that it calls for much more thought. But most of all, you lead them to the hope that there is some way out, some better method, some relief from pressure.

In order to convince or persuade your audience, you will have prepared your speech in much the same way that a debater prepares his case. Through the process of reasoning described in the next chapter, you will appeal to the intellect of your listeners. You will appeal also to their emotions. Love, rightful pride, patriotism, loyalty, devotion may all be areas of appeal. As a persuasive speaker you must use both approaches. If you persuade your audience, they will act willingly; if you force them, they rebel. Persuasion is possible only through reason enriched by emotion. Your audience will respond to you to the degree that you reveal sincerity and integrity as qualities of the inner you.

Speaking is an entertaining art. Perhaps a better word is *interesting*. Completely entertaining speeches are rare, but all speeches should be interesting. You have already been an entertainer of your audience as you held its interest by dispensing new information. You have interested your audience by your deeper consideration as you persuaded or convinced it of new aspects of a known subject.

These are all elements of entertainment. What usually is implied by the term is *humor*. Humor should be included in every type of speaking whether you seek to inform, to persuade, or to convince. Humor has been so overworked and misused that it is sometimes more hindrance than help. Humor should be appropriate. It should fit the occasion and the subject. Humor dragged in for the mere sake of humor calls attention to itself and thereby violates the rules of art. Humor must be harmonious. What is laughable at one time is not so at another, so that humor, as other aspects of speech, must be adaptable. Humor calls for "special handling." All cannot use it effectively. Material that produces spontaneous laughter is true humor. No one can tell you how to produce this magic effect. Humor is a natural outcome of your happy disposition, your light-hearted attitude, your friendly disposition, and your power of observation. Everyday life has enough elements of true humor within it to give you ample material for original humor. Humor may be developed on the spot, from situations that arise in the view of your audience. This is true and genuine humor, for it is spontaneous and fresh.

The process of communication that will take place as you go through the presentation of the speech will certainly change your listeners. As you inform them, impress them, convince them, and entertain them, you will effect a personality change within them. This, in turn, will effect a personality change within yourself.

What will your audience see? Your eyes give you away. They express how you really feel about almost anything. Little goes on in your mind that doesn't show in your eyes. Tests show that when a person looks at something or someone he likes, the pupils of his eyes grow larger. When it is something unpleasant, the pupils contract. Although your audience cannot see your eyes this closely, they do watch your eyes as you speak.

Your eyes are a very important part of your speechmaking. Your listeners listen by watching your eyes. If you are in a very poor light, the audience will find it hard to hear, without know-

Your appearance speaks louder than your words.

ing why. The expression in your eyes is picked up and enlarged by the expression in your facial muscles. Your words are helped or hindered by your eyes and your facial expression.

Poise is that elusive quality that enables you to appear calm and in control even when you do not feel calm inwardly. You are calm by virtue of the fact that you know what you are going to say, and you have practiced how to say it. You may feel some surge of anticipation that gives you extra "charge." This is good. The added energy you feel mounting within you as you see and hear your audience gathering is channeled into extra verve in your speaking. It is similar to special fuel that rockets need for takeoff.

Your audience is aware of your ease and confidence as you walk calmly to the speaker's stand. Reassured, they look forward with added anticipation to what you will have to tell them. The atmosphere of expectancy is mounting. It is like the sparked activity before the rising of a curtain in the theatre.

As you take your place at the podium or speaker's table, remember to stand well. Good speakers never drape themselves over chairs or desks. You are part of the "line" your audience sees. If the line is crooked or disjointed, it is like seeing a picture on a wall hanging at a slant. It is unpleasant to the viewer. Do not lean on anything. Stand, sit, and walk at all times with the agility and grace of a fashion model.

Do not use the microphone unless it is absolutely necessary. You have enough built-in power for most normal occasions. A microphone gives a mechanical ring to natural tones. You are much more effective without one, but be sure your audience can hear you.

Since you are part of the visual image of your audience, your clothing also is important. Subdued colors are in order, with an accent of "sparkle" in a necklace or tie-pin. No jangling earrings or bracelets. The accent should come from your face, hands, movements, and words—not from flashy attire. Distraction from the message would be the result of such poor taste.

What will your audience hear? Be sure your audience *hears,* otherwise the total effort is lost. You must project with all your force without seeming to force. This, too, has been part of your basic training in rehearsal. Audiences today are accustomed to wide-screen Technicolor projection in movies. You have the great responsibility of matching such projection as a speaker! The surprising fact is, you can do it.

Cheerleaders, as well as other rally groups, are good examples of projection. They are heard with impact! What is the secret? They have plenty of air supply, they open their mouths, and push the sound out.

As a speaker, your projection should carry not only volume but beauty and richness of tone as well. Open your mouth wide; place the voice in the mouth and let the tone ring out clear and strong.

Your audience will help you in the production of sound. Sound is much better when there is a "full house." People's clothing and bodies act as sound absorbers. The Greek actors used megaphones built into stage-masks to magnify sound. Megaphones or modern microphones, however, never replace the well-opened mouth, the accurate syllable formation, or the well-projected voice.

A full, rich voice is an asset at all times. It is especially important that a speaker or actor use a strong, clear, flexible, and compelling voice.

Your audience will be satisfied with nothing short of perfect resonance, articulation, pronunciation, flexibility, or power.

Your audience wants to work! Your audience does not enjoy being passive. They expect that, as a good speaker, you will make them work. Enlist their active participation. Make them think, reflect, examine. Obtain their cooperation. Talk *to* them, not *at* them. If you confer *with* them, they will become active and work with you.

Don't make the mistake of giving away the point of your

speech before you reach the end. Keep them working, but keep them guessing, too, if possible.

Remember, your audience is kind. Your listeners want nothing so much as to see you succeed. If you make a mistake, lose something, or fumble for a word, your audience becomes more concerned than you. Make light of it, turn it into a humorous incident, laugh at yourself, and relieve their tension. In this way you increase their response through understanding and a natural sympathy.

Someone has said that the sweetest sound anywhere is the applause of an audience. It is your payment for the long and hard hours you have spent writing and rehearsing. It is the symbol of appreciation for a good presentation.

The surge of joy you will feel as you leave the speaker's platform, the ring of applause in your ear, will give you a thrill that you will never forget. You will want to go back for more. The magic will never wear off. "The pain is over; the beauty lasts." You are on the road to popularity. You have insured your success. You will never give up. There are too many worlds to conquer. There are too many things to say, and too many people waiting to hear them. You are a new and more powerful YOU.

CHAPTER VII

Argumentation and Debate

If you have experienced and enjoyed the simpler forms of speech experiences, you will probably be looking for more difficult and more involved ones.

Argumentation and debate is the form you want. To argue is a time-old practice with you. You began as a baby. When you wanted something, you cried. If you didn't get it, you cried harder. If someone brought you the wrong thing, you turned your head and said "no."

As you grew older, your instinct for argumentation became more refined. You announced to your parents that you would like a new dress, or wished to go to a party with your friends. If they disagreed, you immediately began to supply them with reasons why you should. Usually, your arguments took the form of these expressions:

"All the others are going."
"All the others will have a new outfit."
"You just don't care about me!"

and possibly, tears or banging of doors helped to express your disappointment. The truth of the matter is that possibly each of you was partly right.

As teens, you will want to use reasoning methods more adult than crying, pouting, or banging doors. You will want to learn to debate.

Most prominent public figures use debate as a tool in their public careers. Debate is a skill learned either in junior or senior high school. Debate has a natural place in the upper elementary level of education, for it is at that time of your life, as you approach teenhood, that you become especially argumentative. You want to know the "why" and the "how" and especially you are very vindictive about "why not?" These are the years in which you are really ready to learn the principles of argumentation and logic.

If you have passed through these years and still are not convinced about many things, it is not too late to begin your study of this fascinating and challenging speech activity.

Debate has come in for some very favorable public notice within the past decade, as so many political leaders are again challenging their opponents to public debate. This was a popular form of electioneering in the days of Lincoln. The added dimension of television brings the topic of debate to the general public and has great influence in the election polls.

It may well be part of an electioneering program, for its fundamental purpose is persuasion—nonviolent persuasion. Ballots without bullets.

Franklin Delano Roosevelt used discussion and debate as a medium whereby ideas and evidence were exchanged. This exchange served as a cooperative means for preparation and a supplement to individual research and study. After careful preparation, discussions were held to determine such questions as: What issues should comprise our case? What arguments should be included under each issue? What evidence should be used for each argument?

Differences of opinion arose at these discussions, but compromises were reached through cooperative deliberation and informal argument.

Begin with discussion. Discussion is an activity in which thoughts, ideas, information are circulated freely. From the vast amount available, those items are selected on which you wish

114   The Teenager and Speechmaking and Debating

Speechmaking involves the total YOU—hands, eyes, blend into the act of verbal and visual communication.

to work as part of your organization of ideas . . . to be known as your *case*.

Through cooperative deliberation, debaters use discussion to prepare for debates.

Through discussion and informal argument, they decide on the final case.

Through debate, they become all-out advocates of the side of the proposition they choose to support.

Discussion and debate are good preliminary foundations for many careers in life. Speakers, teachers, lawyers, judges, and diplomats must be skilled in this art.

FDR Used the "Art" of Debate

Franklin D. Roosevelt joined a law firm. When a case was taken he arranged conferences with his client to determine the facts. Next followed conferences with the law firm to see how the case should be pleaded, or presented. Differences arose in the discussions, but through compromise a plan of action was determined. The lawyer sifted the information and selected the most important facts to present the strongest case possible.

Facts are ascertained through discussion.

Through debate, facts are presented for judging.

From the law office many men go on to seek public office. Roosevelt in due time announced his candidacy for the New York Senate. Discussion was again used with campaign managers to get facts. Through sharing information and group problem-solving, the candidate presented his case and answered his opponent's arguments. Discussion and argument are necessary for political debates. The office seeker talked to his coaches or managers to decide how to advance his position. Finally, he used debate when he presented his stand on the issues and refuted his opponent's charges.

Roosevelt won his race for the New York Senate and soon became the leader of a group of eighteen senators.

All through his career, discussion was again used to exchange views on controversial issues.

Discussion and informal argument were used to decide the arguments and strategy for forthcoming debates.

Debate was used to defeat the proposal on the floor before the group who would vote the decision into law.

You as a debater. As a debater, you are a searcher for factual information—a searcher for favorable evidence. Debate is not an "either-or" proposition; a good debater will know both sides. You will know the complete facts, but choose the ones you wish to make use of in presenting a "case."

As a debater you seek objective analysis and understanding; an evaluation of the best arguments on all sides; finally, you become an advocate of one particular side.

A debater is first an investigator, a seeker, an analyzer. You cannot plead a cause unless you know all sides of the question—opposing arguments as well as your own.

Discussion is not a substitute for investigation or research, but instead an added factor in preparation whereby the participants can pool facts and reflective thoughts.

Debates may be grouped as

educational debates
courtroom debates
campaign debates
legislative debates

Debate may be called a conflict-resolving process.

Discussion constitutes the best approach to problem-solving. Realists appreciate that not all conflicts are resolved in this way. Our feelings may be too strong to permit concessions; our personal interests may prevent compromise. Some problems must be submitted to a third party for solution—a jury, a legislative body, an electorate, a judge. These situations call for advocacy; opposing debaters present the case for one side of a question to a third group for decision. The advocate asks: "What are the facts favorable to my cause?" "What are the arguments favorable to my position?"

Thus, the debater on the platform becomes an advocate, not an investigator.

Debate Seeks Peaceful Solution

If methods of communication are not used, or fail, belligerent methods will be employed—labor will strike against management; industry will boycott labor; individuals will resort to mob violence, nations will go to war. Resorting to violence will become less frequent as peaceful methods—discussion and debate—are perfected. A healthy attitude toward problem-solving consists of a high regard for the methods of discussion and debate and active vigilance in seeking ways to improve them.

Studies in discussion and debate are not ends in themselves, but they offer training for life situations of cooperative deliberation and advocacy. To resolve conflicts, skilled arbitrators and advocates become essential. Certain situations demand people skilled in these processes.

Lawyers skilled in cooperative deliberation are very much needed today. That is, they talk to both parties and try to convince one of the truth and integrity of the other party and the claims made by each.

Numerous cases in human affairs are settled through the peaceful means of discussion and debate learned in speech classes or in forensic groups in high schools. One attorney is reputed to have settled more than 90 percent of his cases outside a courtroom through discussion and debate.

Debate is one of the oldest activities of mankind. Calm, orderly debate, in which speakers argue for acceptance of various answers to a given question, is an obvious feature of modern parliaments and congresses.

The early Greeks were firm believers in the art of speech as a basis for democracy. No man, they felt, was a complete man worthy of participating in government unless he possessed the ability to present his "portion of truth." Plato and Socrates are studied today for their instruction in the science and art of argumentation.

Ancient kings maintained councils of nobles to give them advice. When the nobles disagreed, they were allowed to debate their proposals before the king, who acted as the final judge in choosing one or the other plan of action.

In American colonial times, much of the education was conducted orally. Students were not considered "educated" unless they were proficient in skills of oral expression. The young nation called for vibrant and powerful speakers, and students themselves formed out-of-school occasions in which they met to develop and perfect their speaking skills. Debate was one of the areas of exercise. Future laws and government could be formulated only through exercise of the right of "freedom of speech."

Benjamin Franklin, prominent in organizing the school system in Pennsylvania, required that ". . . youth be well instructed in oral language, to be fitted, thus, for any business, trade, or profession." He wanted youth to develop clarity and conciseness, to pronounce distinctly, to form "their own styles." Franklin was aware of the times and its specific needs. He firmly believed in the need for instruction in all forms of speech. He favored and promoted the study of argumentation and debate as a necessary fundamental for the emerging nation. While interested in commerce and trade, he saw the need for a vital "lawyer class" that would steer political ferment during the ensuing decades. He believed, wisely, that the new nation's citizens would be called upon "to speak for themselves" before the tribunals of the world.

Modern democratic societies have looked upon skill in the art of debate as a priceless asset among free men. It is a method that enables any citizen to propose a better plan of action than the one set forth by the ruling power. If the speaker can convince enough of his fellow citizens that he has the better plan, he can literally change the policy of his city, county, state, or nation.

You may be accustomed to the formal debating by members of legislative bodies such as the Senate and House of Representatives. In these houses, elaborate rules are laid out to insure adherence to the two basic rules of debate:

- One issue at a time.
- Equal opportunity for presentation of each viewpoint.

Some propositions are debated in committee, a small group; some are debated "on the floor" before a larger group.

Debate may seem a formal term although actually, you "debate" every day. Every situation in which you find yourself—and there are many—that demands that you compare alternatives, is a situation forcing you to weigh the merits of choices. Sometimes the debating process will take place entirely within yourself; sometimes in the presence of others; sometimes, as in school debates, with other groups and for the purpose of "winning" the decision.

Debating can be a great help to you all your life. If you learn the rules you will be a better thinker, a better organizer, and a more effective speaker. You need not be a lawyer or a congressman. You may be a teacher, a lecturer, an author, a salesman, or an attorney.

Why Debate?

Debate enables you to develop many things, some of which are:

- ability to collect and organize ideas
- ability to evaluate evidence
- ability to see logical connections
- ability to think and speak in outline terms, clearly and convincingly
- ability to adapt

120   *The Teenager and Speechmaking and Debating*

Intense communication indicates imaginative and enthusiastic life.

Debate skill cannot by itself make good citizens, but the American who cannot speak effectively in an organized way is a voiceless citizen, one whose good ideas may be lost in the crowd because they are never heard. Debating can be highly valuable to you and to your country.

Learn the Terms:

Debate: The opposing of arguments on a given proposition between a supporting affirmative and a dissenting negative.

Argument: A reasoning process in which conclusions are drawn from premises.

Brief: A complete, logical outline that organizes and records all the available material on one side of a proposition.

Burden of proof: The duty of making good his claim that rests upon the one who starts an action, who demands a change from the existing situation.

Burden of rebuttal: The responsibility of "continuing the debate."

Case: A complete statement of the position that either the affirmative or negative takes on a proposition *in a given debate*.

Construction: The sum total of the arguments that either affirmative or negative uses to build up or *construct* their case. (*Construction* is opposed to *Refutation*.)

Evidence: Facts, opinions, or statements that give rise to proof.

Fallacy: Either a defect in proof or a type of erroneous reasoning that renders arguments logically unsound.

Issues: The inherently vital points affirmed by the affirmative and denied by the negative, upon the establishment of which depends the establishment of the main proposition.

Outline: A step-by-step development of the main ideas.

Presumption: The advantage of "preoccupation of the ground," which lies in favor of the one defending the *status quo*.

Prima facie case: A case that is logically adequate to establish a high degree of probability in its favor and sufficient to win the argument if not answered.

Proof: A logical demonstration that establishes the truth, justice, or wisdom of a proposition, or the probability that the proposition is true, just, and wise.

Proposition: A judgment expressed in a declarative sentence that the listener is asked to accept.

Rebuttal: The representation of argument and evidence (no new argument may be introduced) after the constructive speech with the purpose of recapitulating and reemphasizing basic previous arguments in order to convince the listener.

Refutation: The destruction of opposing proofs (refutation is not confined to the rebuttal period).

Syllogism: The expression of a form of reasoning in which the third proposition follows necessarily from the first two statements called premises.

About the case. A *debate case* is the complete statement of the stand the affirmative or negative takes on a proposition. It includes the evidence, reasoning, exposition, narration, description, and motivation upon which one side chooses to rest its case. It is not simply an outline; it is the complete discourse.

A *prima facie case* is logically adequate to establish the probability of truth in its favor. The presentation of such a case is the only way to prove a given side of a proposition.

Partitioning the case. By partitioning the case is meant the division of the total speaking activity among the various members of the debate team. The particular partitioning of the case should be pointed out by the first speaker on the affirmative team.

The *first affirmative* defines terms, establishes need for proposed change;

The *second affirmative* proposes the plan and shows that it is applicable and advantageous;

The *first negative* answers arguments of first affirmative and shows "no need for change."

The *second negative* answers the second affirmative and shows disadvantages of the proposed plan.

As in any other speech, the debate case should have an introduction, a body, and a conclusion.

The *introduction* is designed to prepare the audience for the material that is to follow. It should arouse attention by providing a setting for the present argument. It also must: state the proposition, define the terms, point out the issues, and partition the case.

The *body* of the case is the area in which the contentions are proven, arguments developed, evidence presented. As in every speech, this is the heart of the debate case.

The *conclusion* is a brief closing interval in which friendly relationship is reemphasized between speaker and listener concerning the case and its proponent.

Affirmative. The affirmative discharges the burden of proof by logically proving all the issues in the proposition. For this reason, the speakers will not select *too many* ideas. It is better to take a few and clearly explain them than to take so many that you and your listeners are equally confused.

A good affirmative case does not attempt to prove more than is required. Argument is limited to topic and its most essential points.

Duties of the *first affirmative* speaker are definite. If you have that position, you will begin by informally greeting your audience. In your introduction, you will clearly and accurately state the words of the proposition. You will comment briefly on the importance and timeliness of the proposition, attempting to arouse interest and attention. You will strive for an "original" approach —not that used by the everyday debater. A quotation or a startling fact might be an "opener."

You will define terms, clearly and concisely. Some debaters begin with the most important words, then continue with the remainder. All words should be defined. Defining aids clarity and stimulates the thinking process.

List the main ideas you have selected as stepping stones to prove in your presentation as a team.

List the topics it is your share to present.

The body of your speech will begin with your statement of a *need for a change* and the evidence to support it. Evidence may be statistics, facts, quotations, statements of authorities.

Make your first statement, followed by *reason one*. Give supporting evidence. Draw the conclusions. Argue your point. Follow your first statement and conclusion by your second. Give *reason two,* with supporting evidence and arguments. Watch your time limit and use as much time as you need to give as many reasons with proof that your speaking time will allow. But do not forget you still must come to the . . .

Conclusion or summary, a brief restatement of your outstanding facts.

Negative. The negative case should provide a sound, valid argument against the acceptance of the proposition. It is better to concentrate on a few solid arguments than to scatter the attack too widely.

The negative does not know before the debate what the affirmative will propose, except in a general way. There are several standard types of cases, however, which the negative will prepare before meeting the affirmative. As ease is gained in debating the affirmative side, the negative speakers will be able to take on their opposing team's statement with the agility of "impromptu" speakers.

Types of Negative Cases:

The negative team may use a case of *simple refutation.* In other words, negative "listeners" are taking notes of the statements made by the affirmative speakers. From precollected statements and evidence (proof), the negative team will select facts with which to attempt to "destroy" the strength of the affirmative's stand. (There is always enough evidence on both sides to make statements *seem* true.)

The negative team may defend the *status quo*. This type of case argues that the present condition is acceptable and satisfactory; no change is needed.

Another modification of this approach is the status quo with slight modifications. The case admits there are some faults in the present situation, but they are so minor as to be capable of remedy without use of drastic measures. (The affirmative's proposals are the "drastic measures.")

The negative may propose a counterplan. This case admits the need for a change, but it offers an alternate solution that is incompatible with the plan of the affirmative. If the negative proposes such a case, it assumes the burden of proving the desirability of its plan. In other words, a counterplan says in effect: "Not your plan, but our plan." This counterplan should be totally different from the affirmative plan. The negative in this type of case becomes a pseudo-affirmative, with the affirmatives defending their first position and refuting the plan of the negatives.

Check as you go:

First Affirmative Constructive:

_____ 1. Greeting (brief).
_____ 2. Introduction (history, importance, timeliness, etc.).
_____ 3. State the proposition.
_____ 4. Define the terms.
_____ 5. Outline the whole case (both your and your partner's part).
_____ 6. Partition the case (i.e., tell what you will do).
_____ 7. Establish need by argumentation and evidence.
_____ 8. *Summarize* your case.

First Negative Constructive:

_____ 1. Greeting (brief).
_____ 2. Accept or reject terms.
_____ 3. *Summarize* affirmative case.
_____ 4. State negative position (i.e., what type of case).

126   *The Teenager and Speechmaking and Debating*

———— 5. Reply to first affirmative arguments by *issues*—BE CLEAR!
———— 6. Go beyond points raised by affirmative to advance negative case.
———— 7. Summarize what you have done and how weakened affirmative case.

Second Affirmative Constructive:

———— 1. Greeting (brief).
———— 2. *Summarize* affirmative case and negative arguments.
———— 3. Tell what you will do (e.g., reply to first negative, explain plan, show its advantages).
———— 4. Reply to first negative arguments to reinforce your case.
———— 5. Propose and explain affirmative plan.
———— 6. Show practicality of plan, how it meets needs set forth in first affirmative constructive.
———— 7. Show advantages of plan.
———— 8. *Summarize* whole affirmative case.
———— 9. Ask acceptance of affirmative plan.

Second Negative Constructive:

———— 1. Greeting (brief).
———— 2. *Summarize* first negative arguments in opposition to affirmative.
———— 3. Add new evidence and argument to support colleague.
———— 4. Reply to second affirmative by *issues*—BE CLEAR!
———— 5. *Summarize* the entire negative case.
———— 6. Ask for a rejection of the proposition.

First Negative Rebuttal:

———— 1. *Summarize* the debate so far.
———— 2. Restate and reinforce *major* negative arguments.
———— 3. Point out weaknesses of affirmative case.
———— 4. Tell what the affirmative must still answer.
———— 5. *Summarize* your arguments.

First Affirmative Rebuttal:

_____ 1. Restate (*summarize*) the affirmative position.
_____ 2. Reply to any questions or *major* arguments of first negative rebuttal.
_____ 3. Answer *major* arguments of second negative constructive.
_____ 4. Point out what negative has not answered.
_____ 5. *Summarize* your rebuttal arguments.

Second Negative Rebuttal:

_____ 1. Briefly sum up debate.
_____ 2. Reply to points first affirmative said were unanswered.
_____ 3. Restate and reinforce *major* negative arguments.
_____ 4. Point out what the affirmative has not answered satisfactorily.
_____ 5. Ask for rejection of the proposition.

Second Affirmative Rebuttal:

_____ 1. Reply to *major* arguments of second negative rebuttal.
_____ 2. Rebuild entire affirmative case by attacking *major* arguments.
_____ 3. Ask for acceptance of the proposition.

How the "Champs" Won

This is an account written about the debaters of Purcell High School, Cincinnati, Ohio—Ohio state champions for the second straight win! It was written by Jim Healy for Cincinnati's *Enquirer Teen-Ager,* edited by Ruth Voss.

> Regular workouts after school each day and on Saturdays and Sundays! Traveling more than 6,000 miles annually! Spending over 700 hours in research! Olympic training? No, it's just a small part of what goes into making a state champion debate team win another state title.
>
> For the first time in the history of Ohio high-school competition, a school has won the state debate title two years in a row.

Purcell High School's varsity debate team again managed to capture first place in the annual Ohio State Debate Tournament at Columbus, Ohio. The team, led by Steve Rehling, president, supported by Chip Zoller, and backed by Paul Sylvester and Chuck Luken, has again qualified for a try at the national title later this year.

What goes into making a championship team? Chip Zoller feels it was "hard work, much preparation, a different style, and probably most important, a real desire to win!" The team began working on the 1968 resolution as soon as it was announced in spring '67. The proposition—*Resolved: That Congress Should Establish Uniform Regulations for Control of Criminal Investigation and Procedure*—sent them first to law books and Supreme Court decisions. These seemed very uninteresting, but necessary, for a thorough background.

As books and pamphlets, and more books and more pamphlets started to arrive, debate cases began to develop. Paul Sylvester assumed the job as first affirmative speaker, with Steve Rehling as second affirmative speaker. In debate, the affirmative team opens and closes a debate. The team members' principal job is to present a case as a type of answer to the resolution. They must be able to support a case by proof which they have gathered in research.

The negative team was composed of Chuck Luken, first negative, and Chip Zoller, second negative. In actual debate they are prepared to defeat the case presented by the affirmative team.

Know It and Say It

Proof is of the utmost necessity in debating. In assorted files, composed of some 3,000 index cards, were small charts, hundreds of facts, and also the case outline of every team debated this year. This is helpful, for, by studying these cases, the speakers add to their own skill and know what to expect from another team.

The team members feel their success this year was due to good facts and logic, helped by an informal and friendly style of speaking. Casualness seems to appeal to students as well as to judges. The organization of knowledge, as well as the friendly style, was suggested by Brother John Pier, who coached the team for three years.

Equally important on Purcell's varsity debate team is Steve Navaro, the backup man. His job is especially difficult, for he has to be prepared to hold down *any one* of the four positions in case of absence or emergency.

All five students on the team feel they have been helped in their speech skill by debating. Chip Zoller is vice president of Purcell Student Council. The other four members are also active in the Council, and hold membership in other school activities. All of them began debate in their freshman year.

Beginning Was Rough

"At first, it was quite hard to learn to forget yourself and keep your mind on the issue at hand," Chip commented. "We had to learn control of person. Very often you feel like going over and smashing your opponent for his stubbornness or failure to see your point. Control is very important. You have to be able to recognize false, inconsistent reasoning an opponent uses in order to confuse you."

After many long hours of study, research and practice, the team members set out for their first debate. They lost. This was their first step on a long journey—the first stage on the long road to a twice-obtained state championship trophy.

Speechmaking Unimportant?

Some schools find no time or need for training in the arts of speechmaking and debating. Others include such courses or opportunities as "extracurricular."

A recent newspaper article noted the fact that extracurricular subjects are becoming more important on a student's cumulative educational record. First of all, they indicate that he has done more than his share, scholastically, if the activity is one that involves learning skills.

Speechmaking and debating is certainly one of these areas. Students who have achieved ability through this outside exercise are finding that many colleges, especially private schools, are placing more emphasis on a student's extracurricular activities.

An example is cited of an official of Harvard University's admissions office who stated his school now admits a smaller number of applications with extremely high Scholastic Aptitude Test scores. He related that the admissions committee has found that very, very bright students with high test scores are sometimes greater risks as far as being successes in college. He further explained this position by saying that the college looks for a special talent in a prospective student—for instance, he stated that an excellent violinist, promising writer or speaker, or a person who has put out the best school newspaper in a long time, and who have low scores, are often accepted.

The trend today seems to be that colleges look for a certain number of students with varied special talents to make up a well-rounded student body.

While a student should not neglect his grades, it is often pointed out that he should not concentrate on book work completely. Some universities are turning down National Merit Scholars or geniuses who have little talent for anything but studying, admitting the smart student with many activities instead.

Meaningful work and worthwhile activities can be quite an asset to a college applicant. Working on a dance committee, or attending a few meetings of school organizations are not exactly the sort of sparks for which colleges watch. Working on a school newspaper in a responsible position, starring in a dramatic production, or being a champion on a debate team will carry far more weight with an admissions committee.

Since a student's participation in extracurricular activities in high school is a good indication of his desire to achieve, and because these activities are such an important part of school life, it is heartening to see colleges placing more and more emphasis on this segment of a student's record.

Girls as Debaters?

It is generally assumed that teen girls are scatterbrains. That may be a fact. Some girls seem to invite the label, by acting as if they were dedicated to looking or seeming silly. But teen girls, is there any reason why your brain should be for limited use only, or why you should allow boy teens to exceed you in the use of intellect? Tests have proven that girls are as bright as, if not superior to, boys in many respects. Debate in an area in which girls, as well as boys, may become proficient, provided that instruction and practice be followed in learning this art, as in any other.

The opinion long held by the world that anything lavished on the feminine section of humanity is wasted, may be due, in part, to the attitude of girls themselves. Girls often confuse lightness of head with lightness of heart. The need for women in good government; the need for women as foreign ambassadors or in political life; the need for excellent women lawyers, all point up the fact that we need and must have good girl debaters.

CHAPTER VIII

New Worlds Await You

As the late Senator Robert F. Kennedy announced his decision to run for the presidency of the United States, he stated that he wished to do so not "to oppose any man, but to propose new politics." New courses of action can only be plotted by present teens who are versed in the arts of oral communication—speechmaking and debating.

It is for this reason that teens must ask themselves whether they are *terrible* or *terrific*.

"Look out, she's thirteen." "Fourteen should be forbidden." "Fifteen is a fearful age," are some danger warnings heard today.

"I am sixteen, going on seventeen," Liesl sang in *The Sound of Music*.

Seventeen is a thrilling age; eighteen, an exciting one.

Teens may be terrible in the sense of being troublesome—troublesome because they are critical. This age is necessarily difficult and painful to a quite astonishing degree. High-school years may be considered critical because they are, *par excellence,* the years of formation. What constitutes the specially critical nature of the teen years is that they are years of *self*-formation.

It is during this time that the human being normally begins to think and to determine with some degree of independence; when the boy or girl begins to become a distinct and autonomous individual. The individual, at first, is carried, then led; during teen years, directed.

Teen years may be said to be the period when consideration is made of what others have made of you. Much more important is what you will make of yourself. Unfortunately, some errors are irretrievable, even those made in teen years. Life is a handsome thing, but fragile. Teen years are crucial for later, mature life. They are also a period of sharp and almost startling development. This growth takes place along many lines, but not at a uniform rate. The intellect must be developed as well as the emotions. This span of years is critical and difficult. Yet, youth *is* the brightest and merriest era in human life. It is in this period that teens become either *terrible* or *terrific*.

A proper channeling of emotions and a consistent development of talents makes you terrific—or a person who will become a constructive member of society. One of the greatest problems of teens is fear, which causes endless suffering. You especially fear laughter from others for failure. At the same time that fear wracks your being, you have violent yearnings for daring. You fear competition at the same time you long for it. All these forces within you will find effective and purposeful outlets if you allow yourself to develop into a total person through the process of learning to express your thoughts as an accomplished speaker.

Are teens talented? Yes, if they begin to develop the talent early. Say "pocket" to eight-year-old Jean Balukas and—quick as a flash, hazel eyes snapping—she'll ask: "Which one?" A pocket to this pert third-grader is not on a dress—it's a side pocket or a corner pocket on a billiard table.

Willie Hoppe, once called the "Boy Wonder," could easily have learned some tricks from Jean, who has been called both the "Girl Wonder" and the "Little Princess of Pocket Billiards." She learned the game from her father at the age of four on the family billiard table in the cellar of the Balukas home. According to her father, "She could just about see over the table."

But within two years she was impressing enough people with her skill to play exhibition games that led to TV appearances.

She recently played a game against a college president. Was

she nervous? Well, between shots she finished her homework and took a nap.

James Schooter, at 13, writes and draws comic books. "I've read comic books all my life, so I thought I could write one, too," says Jim, who lives in Bethel, Pennsylvania. He had never had an art lesson in all of his 13 years, but had learned from his steelworker father, whose hobby is drawing. Jim's confidence in himself was repaid, however, when he sent his finished comic book in for publication. He received a contract to become an artist-writer. This interest and award seemed to stimulate his thinking ability in other areas. He became a top student in chemistry and worked out a very ingenious project which took a first-place award. Meanwhile, he continues writing comic books.

Carolyn Glyn had three novels published before she was 20. Carolyn came out low man in a name-calling contest with her classmates at a private school in England when she was 11. She was so angry at being tongue-tied that she went home and dashed off a story. She found release for pent-up feelings in a book—her reflection on school life. She had published her first poem when she was 7; then a volume of collected poems, centering about her summertime activities at home or on the beach. Writing runs in her family. Originally interested in art, this teen wrote a book about that. She is writing another book. If she can't make a living out of books, or painting, she has a third trade to fall back on. She works as a telephone switchboard operator. Come to think of it, there might be a book in that, too!

Denise Nessas is a teen queen of the needle. Pretty, brown-eyed Denise is a long-haired brunette from Clifton, New Jersey. At 18, she wants to go into fashion merchandising after college. She loves to ski, enjoys cooking for her family and friends, and sings in her church choir. In other words, she's a typical teen.

Well, not quite. Denise also loves to sew, a talent she's been exercising since she was 8 and one that won her the title of Teen Sewing Queen last fall. In fact, she's always wanted a fashion career but was never sure. When she wasn't going to summer school, she designed and made her complete college wardrobe.

A high-school senior when she was a finalist in the Singer World Style-Maker Contest, she won the opportunity to go to Paris, where she won another title. She also had opportunity to meet other French girls her own age. She was surprised to discover that "We all dress alike." But French girls did not know how to sew. "It must be a great disadvantage," the teen mused; "no opportunity for creative thinking!"

Teens are terrific—if they are active, creative, and constructive.

"Mayor for a Day"

During the annual celebration of Girls' Week in Cincinnati, Ohio, this year, leading teens from fifty-two schools competed for the honor of holding the highest office in the city for a one-day period. Representatives of the highest "girl power" from each high school competed. The title would be awarded on the basis of speechmaking ability. The coveted honor went to Alison Maddux, a junior from Summit Country Day School.

Alison Maddux's winning speech:

What's to Be Done About Dope?

Forty-eight days ago, Mark Lynch, age sixteen, walked the streets of Cincinnati with the same curiosity and excitement of any teen-age boy. But Mark's curiosity carried him too far. Now he is dead from an overdose of drugs. He was found lying on a sidewalk in Mt. Adams right in the heart of our city. Mark's case is the extreme, yet all those who take drugs suddenly find themselves different people, cheating those they love, seeing tears in their mother's eyes.

In January and February of 1967, there were eighteen teens arrested for narcotic charges, while in the same space of time this year the number rose to thirty, as reported by the Vice Control and the Federal Bureau of Cincinnati.

There are some definite signs of drug users. Among these are indications of radical change in appearance, temperament, or attitudes. Frequent use of sunglasses hides dilated pupils, and wearing long sleeves conccals needle marks.

Why would a teen, who has everything to live for, start taking drugs? Easy prey for this situation are those who are frustrated, rebellious, or looking for "kicks." Often they are urged on by pushers who need to sell the dope in order to finance their own addiction.

The problem is becoming so widespread that most of today's teens will be faced with this temptation. Imagine your boy friend or brother crawling into a corner as he writhes in pain from the withdrawal symptoms of drugs. This is not a very pleasant picture, but it is becoming an increasingly realistic one. Thirty-nine of the fifty-two schools in the Cincinnati area have students who are taking drugs. With every passing day, the chance increases that someone you know may take his first steps into the escape that heads nowhere.

What can we do to solve this problem? If each of us will go back to our own Student Councils and incite them to form committees to educate the students about the dangers of drugs, and to work along with the Parent-Teacher Associations to alert the adults to the symptoms of drugs, then the awareness of this problem may help to prevent its spread.

I know because you are here that you are interested in the problems of our city. I know because you are teens that you realize this is our problem. I know that if you care, we can do something about this problem. Please think about it. Please help! Please care!

Careers for Speechmakers

Do you like to give advice? Counseling is an occupation that has become quite important in modern life. No school staff is complete today without a group of *counselors*, specifically trained to handle students' problems. Counseling is a career built especially on your power of communication. You must be an efficient listener as well as a tactful advisor—skills emphasized in the career training of would-be experts.

Speech teachers. There are more people in the world today with a need for speech instruction than there are deaf, blind, crippled, and feebleminded put together. Educators, scientists, parents alike neglect the complicated and involved process of speech-making. Children or teens who do not speak well are ridiculed and humiliated by others and recede into shells of individualism and fear. Teachers of speech are in great demand for the necessary promotion of oral communication.

A stage career? As a lover of language and a craftsman of the spoken word, you can stretch your horizons to imagine yourself in the spotlight on some future stage. You belong to an age when the spoken word of a living performer is "software" fed into the "hardware" of giant electronic machines—radio, television, film.

The rapid growth of television and the concurrent opening of employment opportunities provide possibilities of careers in this huge communications empire. Many television stations are advertising daily for teens to accept scholarships and fellowships in this industry. The Television Information Office, 745 Fifth Avenue, New York, N.Y. 10022, publishes a pamphlet "Television Careers" for anyone interested.

People are won through friendliness expressed through a smile and a simple word. Direct and personal contact through speaking, smiling, or clasping a hand is a deep human experience. "Getting to know you" begins with friendly human communication. It is for this experience that would-be office-holders in our country travel "to the people." The cultivation of the ability to be friendly begins in early childhood through good speech habits, and is built up and perfected through the teen years. Your popularity is measured by your friendly speech.

"To win friends and influence people" you need to come alive, discover your own potential, and begin to use it in a positive, new, oral way. Only dead people don't talk; speaking is a sign of life. Correct speaking and intense communication indicate imaginative and enthusiastic life.

You Are Called to Greatness

If you think of yourself as "just average," you will remain just average. Even this is something to rejoice about. Just average could mean "normal." But don't be complacent. Don't be satisfied with "just average" if you have more than average abilities. The fact is that you have more power than you realize and more ability than you are using now. You are entirely too passive when you should be increasingly more active. You are too intelligent to remain mediocre. Middle-rate achievement will not satisfy you. You are meant for something more. You feel insecure amid the turbulent rush of present-day affairs. For these reasons, you need to rise to greatness. Necessity is always the mother of invention.

"Me a success? That's a laugh!" Does this sound like you? Do you beat yourself down while blaming others for doing so? Success is *not* achieved without great effort, but what is there to keep you from making the effort? Where do you begin? With every opportunity you can seize upon, legitimately, within your reach. Others will help you. It is an amazing fact that if you begin something, others will be attracted to imitate you and to assist you. You will find "kindred spirits"—others who wanted to do the same thing, but didn't know how or where to begin. Yes, you can be a success. Not only you, but hundreds and thousands with you. This is the hope of America!

If America is to be saved, it will not be through military power. It will be through the present generation of 24,000,000 teens—the youth tide covering our land.

Appendix

Speechmaking and Debating: Their Place in Education

These are some comments of teens:
"At my school, no debate club exists. For a few years there was some enthusiasm, but this died because of lack of support. This is sad, for speech seems to be the most neglected area of training through early school years and in high school. Speech was expected to be included in English study. The teacher did devote some time—several weeks—to dull and unfruitful attempts in 'the art of speaking.' The instruction consisted, generally, of a list of 'do's' and 'don'ts.' Little, if any method or imagination was used in presenting this material. The class hated it."

"My greatest speech experience in high school was my membership in the Speech and Drama Club. As a participant in this extra-curricular activity, I was permitted to take part in the senior play. This was the most rewarding experience of my entire twelve years of school. I asked myself and others why it had not been provided earlier in my school life."

"My reaction to the present educational system is that as children and teens we are seen, but not heard in classrooms. I would suggest that an oral program be developed from preschool throughout elementary grades, then built into a strong oral communication course in high school. I cannot understand that in a world so aware of the importance of communication, this is the neglected subject in schools."

"My speech training has not been extensive. Therefore, as a college student I find myself a very ineffective speaker. I suffer very much from stage fright, which I realize is due to my lack of experience in speaking before others. I *know* what I should do to speak well, but because I have never had the occasions to do it, I feel I am very unqualified."

"From a small experience, which was very gratifying, of participation in a school stage production, I developed a taste for acting. On leaving high school, I met other teens who are interested in community productions. We have formed our own troupe of players, comprised of boys and girls who had some taste of stage work during the latter months of high school. We have formed our own company, found a sponsor and director, and spend many happy and profitable hours close to the smell of the greasepaint and the roar of the crowd!"

"Of all my teachers throughout twelve years of school, I found one who spread her enthusiasm and interest in theatre to all the students who went through her classes. As they became alumni they formed an adult group who performed in community theatre. This well-known group owes its origin and its success to the influence of one outstanding and dynamic teacher. We shall never be grateful enough to her for her gift of happiness to so many of us."

"Thank you for inspiring me to become interested in the area of speech. I know I was not a very promising student while a member of your class, but I have a surprise for you. After I left high school, I went to college, and *majored in speech.*"

Speech Experiences in Later Life

Lillian was part of the maintenance staff of a high school in which I once taught. After school, I worked with students on speeches and debate. Communication arts were among "extracurricular" activities. As Lillian swept the halls outside, I often noticed her big brown eyes turned longingly towards the open classroom door. One night she approached me and asked if I would work with her "after hours" when her work was done, and the students had gone home. I heard in that longing voice a desire to become an efficient speaker. I knew that the art of speech would help to lift her, like Eliza Doolittle, out of the mop-and-dustpan stage. I assured Lillian I would be happy to

APPENDIX 141

work with her. She wanted a dramatic piece. I had just made a cutting of *The Miracle Worker* from the play. One of the sophomores had taken first place with her rendition of it in a district speech tournament. Lillian took the script home with her that night and read it over. The next evening, when all was quiet, she went through the lines with me. Her deep, rich voice and the experiences she had had through an unhappy marriage and the responsibility of two fatherless children to bring up, added a deep dimension to her vocal rendition. As she finished her last word, "Water!" as spoken by Helen Keller in the cutting, I could hardly refrain from tears—her delivery was so touching. Lillian learned and gave the selection at many women's clubs in the city and finally joined a speakers' bureau. She no longer works as a maintenance person. This is an extract of a letter I received from her recently:

"Lately, I have been doing quite a bit of speaking. Last Friday I spoke to a large assembly on the topic, 'The Negro Woman.' With your direction, I had written and rehearsed it entirely myself. I did quite a bit of research in the preparation. I am still giving *The Miracle Worker*. It is always a favorite. My latest audience was a federated literary club. I enjoyed doing it for the hundredth time, and they were delighted with it. I have spoken before several Head Start groups explaining the function of Head Start and the role of the parents in the program. For the coming year I have been elected vice president of our speakers' bureau. I will be a representative speaker before a national convention this summer. I have chosen as my topic, 'The Lost Art of Doing Nothing.' I am working on it now so that it will be worthy of my audience. There will be many men in the group, so you see it has to be good. I have many other interesting speaking engagements. Thank you for starting me on my career as a speaker. It is much more rewarding than pushing a broom. My latest challenge is speaking to poverty-stricken groups. Being 'hard-put' myself, I can speak in their terms; but thank you for helping me to be able to speak to them and to the other wonderful audiences I have had."

Testimony from those who have experienced speech training and its effect upon later life is, indeed, convincing.

Another student, Judy, writes:

I had always wanted to work in the field of communications from my earliest years. As a sophomore in high school, I had begun to develop my talent in writing. I was so shy, however, I hardly ever spoke in class. All my thoughts stayed right there on my written paper. A turn of events changed me from a timid, scared little creature to the person I am today. I met a teacher who trained me in speech. She looked at one of my written themes, had it published in the school paper, and most wonderful of all—invited me to "say" it before the high-school speech club meeting. Truly, I was "scared stiff." From this tiny beginning, this teacher coached initial efforts of mine in writing for the *original oratory* section of the city speech league. After I wrote the speech, she coached me in it during many long hours after school. I won a first-line trophy on my first try! My hands shook so hard I had to clasp them in front of me. Cold perspiration trickled down my back, but I was determined to win. It wasn't easy, but it WAS worth all the effort. From that first experience, other efforts in the world of speech were easier. I wrote more. I spoke often. I came out of my shell. I felt like a prisoner of war set free—from myself and my crippling fear of a crowd. I increased in vocabulary power, broadened my outlook and took a new interest in life. My teacher made me a student assistant. I coached underclassmen in their speech efforts. I learned to train others. I learned from younger students and they learned from me. It was a real big-sister relationship. In my senior year, I never would believe that as a freshman I could not speak a word. By this time, I had decided on a career in speech arts.

From my beginning efforts in speech, I joined debate and drama groups during high-school and college years. I played one full summer of summer stock, and worked in "little theatre" during the winter. I became a speech teacher at a modeling school. I worked with young children between the ages of 3 and 10. I taught them creative drama, expressive pantomime. From these topics, I advanced them to assigned compositions of 3 or 4 spoken sentences. Thus, I initiated them early into a 2-3 minute "extemporaneous" speech. With teens and adults, I included a topic of current events each week. Speech, I found, opened up the shy student and tamed down the "blowhard" who just talked. Talking had rules which the "blowhard" had to follow, and which really channeled her blowing effectively. This career was entirely possible to me only through, and because of, the push I had received from my "extracurricular" speech experiences in school. Speech has long been my favorite among all my subjects. Through it, I learned to write better themes—better because they told more and told it more vividly. My rambling essay answers on tests became concise and factual, thanks to my debate training. Most important of all was the change in my personality. From a frightened introvert, I became quite outgoing and equal to any situation in speaking. I became a member of a speakers' bureau and an officer in a civic association. I joined literary groups and became a discussion leader in literary reviews. In short, speech training has opened a new door to me—a door which has led to a richer and fuller adult life.

As a bride, I can continue speech interests at the same time I maintain a home for my husband. I am, at present, doing voice-taping work, narrations, announcements, radio and TV commercials. These activities have taken me to various cities throughout the United States and Europe. The results have been highly profitable, both financially and personally. I work in community theatre also. The programs produced by my confreres are of the better type—not the cute, little frilly nothings done by amateurs, but the better classical, deeper reflections on life. My speech training has initiated me into all these possibilities.

My advice to teens in school who do not enjoy a speech course is—FIND ONE. I would like to tell them that they DO have talent, but if it is not used, they will lose many wonderful and rich opportunities. As for careers in speech, they, too, are never mentioned in school, but are opening up at a fantastic rate every day—careers in radio, television, filming, lectures, business speakers' bureaus, civic opportunities, teaching, recording and many, many more.

Thanks to my training in speech, I can now maintain my home and work part time at speech-career work with more financial recompense and with greater personal enjoyment than I could if I pounded a typewriter in an office for a full day!

Is it a fairy tale? It sounds like one, but every word is true. How do you know? Perhaps you have seen me yourself on one of your favorite TV commercials. This could be YOU. Why not?